Wicked YPSILANTI

JAMES THOMAS MANN

Charleston · London

THE
History
PRESS

Published by The History Press
Charleston, SC 29403
www.historypress.net

Copyright © 2014 by James Thomas Mann
All rights reserved

First published 2014

Manufactured in the United States

ISBN 978.1.62619.335.2

Library of Congress CIP data applied for.

Contents

Acknowledgements

I wish to express my gratitude to those who helped made this work possible. I am grateful for all the help I received from the Ypsilanti Historical Society: President Al Rudisill, Archivist Gerry Pety, George Ridenour and Deirdre Fortino. I am also grateful for the help I received from the Archives of Eastern Michigan University: Archivist Alexis Braun Marks, CA; John Clark; and Courtney Donburg. As always, I am grateful for all the help I received from the staff of the Bentley Library, University of Michigan. The proofreading was done by Lauren Thompson, for which I am grateful.

First Murder

George Washburn was a butcher by trade who had lived in Ypsilanti for a number of years. He was said to have been a man of rather coarse make and addicted to alcohol, "cruel and inhuman in his dealings with the lower animals; rude and cowardly in his intercourse with men; a low dastard with women," noted Chapman's *History of Washtenaw County.* No one, then, was surprised when, on February 28, 1860, his wife, Lucy, filed a bill of divorce against him. She charged him with personal violence, drunkenness and adultery. In March, the two separated and lived apart, but George would occasionally visit. He tried to persuade her to quash the bill, but Lucy was determined to be rid of him.

George stopped by the house where Lucy lived, at the southeast corner of North and River Streets in Ypsilanti, on Monday, May 22, 1860. He is said to have been drunk at the time of the visit. George later said he left the house at about 2:00 p.m. Witnesses said he left about 4:00 p.m.

That afternoon, after George had left, James Washburn, the seven-year-old son of the couple, returned home from school. He searched all through the house for his mother but failed to find her. Then he looked down the stairs to the cellar. There he found the body of his mother at the bottom of the stairs.

The *Weekly Michigan Argus* of Friday, May 25, 1860, reported:

> *Upon the discovery of the body an examination of it and the house disclosed these general features: The dress and hair of the deceased were somewhat disarranged; one of her shoes was found in a bedroom, the other she had on her foot; there were*

appearances of blood about the nose and mouth, and marks as of the grasp of a hand on the throat and neck and some other immaterial bruises. In the bedroom spoken of there were two beds. One of them was disarranged, but perhaps no more so than might have been left by being turned over for airing, on the under side of the tick of the feather bed were found spots of apparently fresh blood, and there were appearances about the room that might indicate that a struggle had taken place; one or two small plaster images were found broken.

After the discovery of his wife's body, George was found in the hotel room where he boarded. When found, he was in bed and, perhaps, asleep.

An inquest was held the next day by Justice Cook and a jury impaneled. The jury returned a verdict of "death by violence from some person or persons to them unknown."

The *Detroit Free Press* of Tuesday, May 23, 1860, reported, "The generally accepted theory is that Mrs. Washburn was murdered either by her husband or some one else; that she was strangled in the bed to which allusion has been made, and her body placed where it was found to make it appear that she came to her death by a fall down the steps."

This was the first murder to be committed in the city of Ypsilanti.

The case went to trial in the circuit court on June 19, 1860, and lasted two days. At the trial, the prosecution called James Washburn, the son of George and Lucy. Counsel for the defendant objected, on the grounds that at seven years of age, he was too young. Defense claimed the boy had been tampered with by his grandfather, James H. Young. The court overruled the objections, and the boy was sworn in.

Before the boy was sworn in, the judge asked if he knew it was wrong to tell a lie. The boy said yes and that he would be punished if he did but did not say how he would be punished. Under questioning, James said his grandfather, who had brought him to the trial, had told him he must say his father had murdered his mother.

During the trial, the prosecution offered in evidence what it said was a warrant issued in a criminal case against George Washburn by Justice of the Peace D.B. Greene. Defense objected on the grounds that the warrant was irrelevant and immaterial. The prosecution then called D.A. Wise to the stand, as he was the constable who had served the warrant on Washburn. Constable Wise testified, "I reside in Ypsilanti; am a constable and was in March last; I served the warrant here produced on Washburn in March last, at Mooreville, and arrested him; told him contents of warrant; I don't remember of reading the warrant to him."

Under cross-examination, Wise said, "I was employed by Joslin to go after Washburn; I never made any return on the warrant I never took Washburn to the office of the justice who issued the warrant; I took him to Joslin's office; I supposed the matter adjusted between Washburn and his wife; I let him go on my own responsibility; supposed the matter was settled; never arrested him again on the warrant."

The prosecution entered the warrant into evidence to show the bad relations between George Washburn and his wife. The subject of the warrant and the reason for it being issued were never entered into evidence. The subject of the warrant or criminal charge was not given then or later.

The only questionable point in the case was whether the murder was premeditated. The jury considered the case all night before returning a verdict of "guilty of manslaughter" on June 21, 1860, and recommended Washburn to the mercy of the court. Judge Lawrence sentenced him to twelve years in the state prison.

The case was appealed to the Michigan State Supreme Court on July 30, 1860. The defense claimed that a witness who was seven years of age was not competent to testify. The defense further claimed that the testimony concerning the warrant served against George Washburn should not have been admitted into evidence. The case was heard by the court on May 3, 1861, and decided on July 17, 1861. The court ruled that a child of seven years of age was competent to testify and stated that the question of his credibility was for the jury to decide.

On the warrant, the court ruled "that evidence of this fact was admissible, as tending to show hostile relations existing between the prisoner and the deceased, which would bear upon the question of motive, and tend to prove malice. And it being made to appear, by the cross-examination, that the arrest was for an offense upon the wife, the error of admitting evidence of an arrest, without showing for what was thereby cured."

"The guilty wretch served a term of years," noted Charles Chapman in his *History of Washtenaw County*, "enjoying the hospitality of the State immensely, and actually returned to the scene of his crime unabashed; made a short stay among a people who loathed him, and leaving, went into the world who knew him not."

The house where the murder was committed has long since been demolished. Today, it is the site of the octagon house, home to the SOS Crisis Center, which helps people in need, including women who are victims of abuse.

Chapter 2

Dead Man Alive

The American Civil War began in 1861, and as the first shots were fired, a call went out to the young men of the nation to take up arms to save the Union. In every community, including Ypsilanti, many young men answered the call. For some, the war would be a grand adventure, a break from the dull life they had known. For others, it would be an experience of horror that would leave them scarred for life. Then there were those who never returned home because they gave their lives for the cause. For the families of those who died, there would remain an empty place in their lives, as well as questions that most likely were never answered. Did their son or brother die in battle with courage and valor? Then again, did he die of illness in torment and pain because of poor sanitation? For many, there would always be a doubt, a hope, however faint, that the loved one did not die but still lived and would one day come home. After the war, there were those who were willing to exploit that hope for their own profit.

On January 23, 1869, the *Ypsilanti Commercial* carried the following item:

> *A circumstance of thrilling interest is on the tapis* [sic] *just now—one of those strange incidents connected with war times. A son of a widow in our city was reported killed during the late war. After the close of the war, his death was announced circumstantially by his companions in arms. They assisted burying him. One of our citizens on a visit south says that he saw him and that he is alive and well. It is surprising however, that he should*

fail to communicate with his friends here. It is asserted that his mother is drawing a pension on account of her deceased son.

The next issue of the weekly *Ypsilanti Commercial*, on January 30, 1869, carried a statement from someone who was "somewhat connected in regard to the aforesaid rumor." The author further stated that there was "another rumor, in which I am more directly brought into public conversation." The author chose not to give his name. The statement began with a claim that the men from the northern United States were being held in southern prisons not because of any crime they may have committed but because they were Yankees.

Details are not necessary. Examine the records or annual reports of Southern Prisons and you will find that over seventy per cent of the inmates are young men; young men "who have fought for their country, and in defense of the stars and stripes."—Young men who sought labor among people whom they thought to be upright, honorable, and hospitable. Alas! For the honor—it fell with the confederacy, and the consequences are that many of our Northern boys are incarcerated within the walls of Southern prisons. And what has sent them there? Is the commission of some crime? This is frequently the case. But alas! It is too often otherwise; and through prejudice and dastardly hankering for revenge, the innocent are punished with the guilty. I speak from personal knowledge, and would say to the friends of the young man in question, that they need consider it no disgrace that he is on a Southern prison.

That he was alive a short time since I had proof. It fell to my lot not long since to be introduced into a certain building and informed that I could reside there without charge, with privilege of Shop of work.

It appears that said "dead man" had been and was, still living in another part of the same enclosure, by some means he was afterwards brought and placed in the same Shop where my daily attendance was required. The sequel in this—matters transpired that I ought not to be there, and was accordingly released from all further responsibilities, he remains there for a short time. My being non-conversant upon the subject heretofore was by his special request.

To this was added a P.S.: "In a communication just received, the keeper seems to throw a blind over the matter—acknowledging that a person by the same name is there, but is not the person whom we represent. We may be mistaken, but if so, it is miraculous to us."

Nothing more was heard of the matter until March 20, 1869, when the *Ypsilanti Commercial* published a story of some length by Ann Ellwell, the mother of the man supposed to be alive in a southern prison. She wrote that the men who reported her son alive were John Putney and his son Samuel. "They are very—*very* positive," wrote Mrs. Ellwell. She continued:

> *Mr. John Putney having visited the South immediately upon his return, called on me for the express purpose of informing me that my son was alive. He then said: "I cannot be mistaken, Mrs. Ellwell, as I saw him and talked with him. He requested me not to tell you." He then says, "Had you been a father, I never should have told you; but a Mother, I considered it a parent's duty to come and tell you."*

She noted that in the article authored by Samuel Putney he admitted he was confined in the same prison as the man he later claimed was her son but did not say for how long he was confined there or why he was incarcerated. "We think," she wrote, "if they imprison *falsifiers* down South they 'hit the mark' when they caught *him*."

William Ellwell was, as best his mother could recall, about five feet, ten inches tall; had very light hair, light eyes and complexion; would have been twenty-nine years of age in 1869; and had a fair education. The keeper of the prison responded to an inquiry by Mrs. Ellwell to say there was a prisoner there by the same name. "He is well; is registered from Ohio, 21 years of age no education; temperate, and single—5 feet, 6½ inches high, weighs 148 lbs. fair complexion, dark hair and eyes, woman tattooed on right arm."

Mrs. Ellwell continued her account with a letter from a J.T. Bernard that read:

> *The facts pertaining to Ellwell's death are, as near as I can remember, that in August, 1864, our whole regiment became engaged in battle, and during said time poor Billy …, Henry Carpenter and Pascal Odette were killed; and what makes me think there is a falsehood somewhere is the fact that although I did not help carry either off the battlefield, I helped dig their graves,…helped put them in, cut their names, rank and regiment, date and cause of death, on a piece of board, and put it at their heads…They were buried side by side, William on the right. I notified Mrs. Ellwell of the fact, and sent her a lock of hair from each, and, I think a sister of Henry's named Elsie, wrote an answer…Even if Billy had lived, I know that could never have committed an act which would send him to the*

Penitentiary:—He was a very intimate friend of mine, and as far as I am capable of judging human nature, I know that he was an honest, upright and honorable young man.

Mrs. Ellwell included a letter by Henry Davis, who had been a captain in the Fourteenth Michigan Volunteers:

Having heard a report circulated by some person in Ypsilanti, that your son William is alive, and in prison in one of the Southern States, I have to say that it is false. Having been acquainted with your son several years previous to his enlistment in the 14th Regiment of Michigan Volunteers of which regiment I was a member from its first organization, until mustered out of the service at the close of the war; and I can testify that he was killed in action on the 8th day of August, 1864, near Atlanta, Georgia; furthermore, I saw him after he was shot, and when he was buried. He was a good soldier and respected by his officers and beloved by his comrades.

These are facts that can be testified to by his Company officers and several of his comrades now living in Detroit and Ypsilanti...What object any person should have for circulating such a false report, is beyond my comprehension.

The object Samuel Putney and his father had in circulating a false report of William Ellwell being alive in a southern prison was most likely financial. The two most likely concocted some plan to trick money out of Mrs. Ellwell in the hope of saving her son from prison. As it turned out, Mrs. Ellwell was too smart for them and foiled their plan.

Evidence for this opinion is supported by the fact that Samuel Putney was arrested in Flint in February 1872 on a charge of procuring money under false pretenses. Then, in March 1877, he was tried in the Washtenaw County Circuit Court on several charges of forgery. He was convicted and sent to the prison at Jackson for ten years.

Chapter 3
Temperance War of 1873

The city of Ypsilanti had been thick with rumors and threats of violence the week before Friday, July 18, 1873. Nothing more, however, was expected than the hanging of effigies and the placing of coffins in front yards. Instead, it was one of the most exciting and event-filled weekends in the history of the city.

On that Friday night, a dwelling house on Prospect Street, occupied by a George Wells, his wife and two other families, was attacked by men armed with clubs. In an instant, seven windows were smashed. A Mr. Bates and his wife were sleeping near a front window when the glass was smashed. The couple was awakened with the thought that the Day of Judgment had just arrived. The two sprang from their bed, and Mr. Bates set off in pursuit and ran out of the house. Once outside, Mr. Bates looked around, but there was no one to been seen. The front gate and a large gate leading into an alley were left open.

Seven windows had been smashed: four windows on the front of the house and three on the north side of the house. Under each of the seven windows was found a club. "We have one of these clubs in our possession, large around as a man's wrist, three feet one inch long, bowed at one end, while the other forms a handle, the bark being neatly trimmed off with a draw shave—making a solid stick. This is a face simile [*sic*] of the other six— well adapted to their mischievous mission," reported the *Ypsilanti Commercial* of Saturday, July 26, 1873.

As to the motive for the attack, the *Ypsilanti Commercial* noted that a resident of the house, George Wells, had testified in a suit against a local

Ypsilanti mayor Watson Snyder was determined to see that the ordinances concerning the liquor traffic in the city were enforced. *Courtesy of the Ypsilanti Historical Society.*

liquor dealer. Men had come around the house the previous Sunday and made threats against anyone who served as a witness against a liquor dealer. After the attack on the house, Wells left town, and he was to have been an important witness in a case against a liquor dealer the next Tuesday.

Liquor was seen by many in the nineteenth and early twentieth centuries as an evil, causing most of the social ills of the time, such as drunkenness, which caused men to neglect their families, as fathers spent their wages on drink instead of caring for their wives and children. A temperance movement in Ypsilanti arose to oppose the liquor dealers, calling for the enforcement of the ordinances regulating the hours of operation of the saloons. For some time, the local authorities had been negligent in the enforcement of these tenets. In large part due to the temperance movement, Watson Snyder was elected mayor of Ypsilanti in April 1873. Once in office, Snyder brought about the enforcement of the ordinances regulating the liquor dealers, and soon some were taken to court and fined for being open on Sundays. A reaction from the liquor dealers was to be expected.

The night after the attack on the house on Prospect Street, Saturday, July 19, Justice of the Peace Crane told his family that he felt in his bones that some mischief was brewing. He took the precaution of preparing himself by some means of self-defense.

That same night, someone broke into the offices of the justice and the city clerk and then, in the same room in the Moorman Block, carried off books, papers and records and some eleven hundred chattel mortgages. The desk of Justice Crane was broken open and all its contents taken. "The docket embracing recent liquor suits, was in the table drawer, and overlooked," reported the *Ypsilanti Commercial*.

This is an undated photograph of an unidentified saloon. This saloon was typical of the 1800s. This was the den of evil the temperance movement sought to close. *Courtesy of the Ypsilanti Historical Society.*

Among the items taken was a Bible that Justice Crane had used in court for twenty years. Justice Crane said it was his prayer that the Bible would become a "lamp to their feet and a light to their path."

The thief of the documents would not be discovered until the next Monday.

For some time, Lee Hendricks and his wife feared there would be an attempt to set fire to the Methodist church. "They have taken the precaution, after turning off the gas, of opening the window blinds in their bedroom, and removing the curtain. The room being on the north side of the house, nearly opposite the lecture room of the church. The head of the bed being towards the south," noted the *Ypsilanti Commercial.*

Mrs. Hendricks awoke between the hours of one and two o'clock in the morning of Monday, August 21. She was surprised to see the room well lighted. At first she thought the gas lamps had been left on. As she rose up, she looked out the window and saw flames bursting out of the lecture room door of the church. At once she screamed, "Fire!"

The Methodist church as it appeared in 1873. *Courtesy of the Ypsilanti Historical Society.*

Her scream awoke her husband. She sprang from her bed, put on what clothing was at hand and ran for a pail of water. At the door of the church, she tossed the water through a hole in a lower panel of the door. Then she picked up a stick and tried to break through the door. Her husband was soon at her side and battered down the door. All the time, the two cried, "Fire!" Help soon arrived, and with a few pails of water, the fire was put out.

The cause of the fire was then discovered. "Kerosene had been put through a hole bored in the door, poured into the room in sufficient quantities to saturate the carpet, and then set on fire. It is probable that the sudden explosion of the kerosene awakened Mrs. Hendricks," reported the *Ypsilanti Commercial.*

At the time of the fire, a strong northwest wind was blowing. The flames, if not put out when they were, could have spread from the church and burned a large part of the city. After all, this is what would happen later in the year in Chicago.

The question everyone asked was, who was behind all this? The liquor dealers were suspected for the smashing of windows, but it did not seem likely that they would steal the court and city records and set fire to the Methodist church. After all, these actions would result in a backlash against them.

The *Ypsilanti Commercial* reported:

> *Some believe that the stealing of the City and Justice Records was done by outside parties who had reward in view, and plunder. Since Mr. N. Cordegy's and other residences on and near Cemetery Street (Prospect Street) were broken into and robbed that night. Supposing that the fire was a certainty, they began at this distant point, expecting to make a bigger thing as the fire progressed, and the people vacated their homes. If this theory of the fire is true, the perpetrators have picked up their traps and are far away. But why, at this juncture, the fire and the raid upon the Justice documents? This the reader can answer as well as we can. It is said that unknown persons have been seen prowling around our city of late, receiving mail matter under different aliases. Since the fire, they have left the city.*

The Ypsilanti City Council held a regular meeting on the evening of Monday, August 11, the day the records from the office of the clerk were discovered to be missing. The minutes of the meeting, published in the *Ypsilanti Commercial* of August 16, noted, "On motion, the Mayor was instructed to expend the sum of $60 to employ a diver to search the river bottom for the records and books supposed to be there."

A lot of excitement for a small city to experience in one weekend, but there was more to come.

Burning of the Gymnasium

Physical education, consisting of gymnastics and calisthenics, was provided at the Michigan State Normal School, now Eastern Michigan University, in a primitive and unpretentious building behind the main building of the school. On the night of August 1, someone entered the building and poured kerosene about. Then this was set on fire.

When the fire was discovered, the gymnasium was a sheet of flames. There was a risk of the fire spreading to the main building of the school. The burning of the school may have been the intent of those who had set the fire, as the wooden walkway between the buildings was said to have been smeared with lard and kerosene. The fire was prevented from spreading to the main building by the pouring of water from the cupola of the main building. As it was, the cornice and rear wall of the main building were badly scorched. The gymnasium was a total loss.

"The building has been a nuisance for years. It was built of wood, and is a good riddance," noted the *Ypsilanti Commercial* of Saturday, August 9.

"About half past ten Saturday night, flames were seen issuing from a barn owned by Mr. McCullough, opposite Follett's Mill. Before anything could be done, the fire had gained considerable headway, and had communicated itself to the large store house, owned by the Deuble Bros…The whole was burned to the ground," reported the *Ypsilanti Commercial*.

The next night, Monday, a barn on Adams Street was set on fire by saturating a pile of split wood with kerosene. Those who were there to start the fire were scared away when a boarder returned home from Detroit.

On the evening of Wednesday, August 6, a man named Myron Brown was arrested and charged with setting fire to the Methodist church. Brown faced examination before Justice Crane on the afternoon of Friday, August 15. "The office," noted the *Ypsilanti Commercial*, "is crowded to suffocation."

The examination was continued on Saturday morning when a Spencer C. Drake, constable second judicial district and deputy sheriff, was called as a witness. Drake said on the evening of July 20, before the theft of the city records was discovered, he was standing in front of Sage's Livery when Brown said he wanted to see him. Drake said he had known Brown for about a year. Brown asked him if he took any stock in the liquor suits. Drake said he did not.

Brown, according to Drake, said he guessed the suits were about played out. Brown then told Drake that the night before, he and three other good square boys had gone to the office of Justice Crane. They broke the door

Left: Joseph Estabrook was principal of the Michigan State Normal School, now Eastern Michigan University, in 1873 and supported the temperance movement. His support of the temperance movement may have been the reason someone tried to burn the school down. *Courtesy of Eastern Michigan University Archives, Ypsilanti, Michigan.*

Below: The Michigan State Normal School as it appeared in 1873. The building behind the school is the gymnasium. This is the only known photograph to show the gym. *Courtesy of the Ypsilanti Historical Society.*

open, and then Brown went into the office alone. Brown told Drake he took all the books and records he could find, which made a heavy load for him. The three others helped him once he was outside the office.

The three carried the books and records to the river, placed them in a sack and threw them in the river. The sack did not sink. Brown then stripped and went in the river and pulled the sack out of the water. The three went to the foundry, where they picked up about one hundred pounds of old iron. This they attached to the sack and tossed it into the river just above the iron bridge. Now the sack sank at once.

Brown then told Drake they intended to burn the Methodist church that night between the hours of one and two o'clock in the morning.

Drake, after hearing what Brown had to say, went to the home of James M. Forsyth, an attorney, but he was not at home. Drake went home and told his father what Brown had said. The two men could not place any credence in the story.

On Monday morning, Drake went to the saloon of Gary Spear, where he found Brown, who was a partner of Spear. Drake asked Brown why he made such a failure of burning the Methodist church. Brown answered that someone discovered the fire before it got fairly underway. Drake asked what kind of auger he used to make the holes in the door, and Brown responded that he used the kind used for beer barrels.

Drake told the mayor and prosecuting attorney what Brown had told him before a reward was offered.

On the Wednesday before the examination, a submarine diver arrived from Detroit. The mayor had sent for the diver to search the section of the river where Drake said Brown had told him the stolen documents were sunk. That morning, the diver searched the channel just below the iron bridge, where he found a coffee sack containing the missing papers.

"He informed the mayor of his good luck, and in the afternoon he went into the water, cast a rope around the sack, and made a motion and it was dragged to the east shore, amid the most intense excitement, the crowd following. The mayor was present with a carriage, and conveyed the sack with its contents to Edwards, McKinstry & Vaueleve's Dry Kiln," reported the *Ypsilanti Commercial* on Saturday, August 16.

There was a great deal of interest in this man Brown and what kind of person he was. "Brown is a fine appearing young man," reported the *Ypsilanti Commercial*, "under 30, tastily, but not foppishly dressed, rather a restless eye. By his friends said to be reticent, scarcely ever known to indulge in boisterous talk, or to communicate his plans and purposes to others. He

Myron Brown was employed as a bartender at the Ypsilanti House at 8 South River Street. This photograph was taken years later, when the building was known as the Congress Street Hotel. *Courtesy of the Ypsilanti Historical Society.*

has been married less than a year. His wife is said to be a very worthy woman." The account further noted, "For the evidence demonstrates that Brown has not only a very wicked place in his heart, but a very soft spot in his head."

At the end of the examination, Justice Crane set bond at $5,000, the lowest amount he said he could conscientiously set it at. As Brown was unable to secure this amount, he was lodged in the county jail. Once Brown was arrested, the setting of fires in the city ended.

Myron Brown stood trial in the circuit court in September 1873 on the charge of setting fire to the Methodist church. On this charge, he was acquitted.

"All accounts agree that Brown conducted himself very gentlemanly and won the confidence and good wishes of the lawyers, jurymen and bystanders," reported the *Ypsilanti Commercial* of Saturday, September 20. Two members of the jury, the account noted, admitted they believed Brown guilty of the charge but felt the evidence was not strong enough for conviction.

Brown was still in the courtroom when he was arrested on the charge of stealing the records of the city. He was released on bond of $3,500. On the second charge, he was also acquitted, the case coming to trial in May 1874. Florence, the wife of Brown, died of tuberculosis on November 18, 1874, at the age of twenty-two.

ACCOUNTING OF JUSTICE WARNER

At the city council meeting of August 11, Albert Crane, the city attorney, submitted a report on the bill of costs submitted by Justice of the Peace Martillo Warner in the suit *City of Ypsilanti v. Martin*. Attorney Crane reported he had "found the bill erroneous in several respects."

Crane listed a number of items in the bill that were in error, including "the charge of $3.36 for swearing 56 witnesses is incorrect, there were only 38 witnesses sworn in all the trials of this case as I have been informed by a member of the Council who was present at the several trials and kept minutes of the proceedings and on that basis the charge should be $1.90, the next item 'to four jury trials $4.00,' is correct; the charge of $25.00 for taking 250 folios of testimony is incorrect, being too large by 200 folios, and the charge should be to taking 50 folios testimony, 10 cents a folio, $5.00."

At the next meeting of the city council, on August 25, the mayor made a number of charges against Justice Warner. One, that Justice Warner had not complied with the city charter by reporting on oath to the council the names of all those on whom judgment had been rendered and all money received from fines. The money from fines was to be paid to the city treasurer quarterly. Second, that Justice Warner did on July 7 render an extortionate bill of costs to the council in the suit instituted by the city against Joseph Martin for violation of the Sunday ordinance. The bill submitted to council amounted to $128.33, and the legal fees were about $60.00. Third, that on July 7, Justice Warner refused to grant a warrant against Myron Brown on the charge of burglary, making it necessary to institute a suit against Brown in Ann Arbor.

Mayor Snyder asked the council to appoint a committee to investigate the charges and examine the docket of Justice Warner of the previous two years. The council agreed, and a committee was appointed.

This was part of the minutes of the city council published by the *Ypsilanti Commercial* on Saturday, August 30. That same issue of the *Commercial* included a Justice Court Report from Warner, concluding with the statement: "In relation to the accusations of Watson Snyder, the Mayor, against me in not rendering a true account of fine moneys, I do not intend to enter into any newspaper prattle with him. I intend to show him up in the Circuit Court, when the people of this County can see who is at fault."

At the meeting of the city council of September 10, a motion was made and adopted that Warner be "instructed to report to this Council at the next meeting thereof, the number and name of every person against whom judgment has been rendered for violation of any of the City Ordinances, as required by Section 56 of the City Charter." Warner appears to have complied with the request but not in a way that satisfied the council. At the meeting of the council on October 6, a motion was made and adopted to return the report to Justice Warner, "with instruction to report on oath the number and names of every person against who judgment has been rendered."

The matter was referred to the Washtenaw County Board of Supervisors, Committee on Criminal Claims, which made its report at the meeting of supervisors on November 8:

> *Upon examining the County Treasurer's books, we find Mr. Warner has paid into the Treasury the sum of forty-six dollars as fine money, and upon examination of Mr. Warner's docket, we find that he has received the sum of $96.00 for fines, and we have evidence at our command which is convincing to us that he has now in his possession a large amount of fine moneys belonging to this county. We also find some twenty-five cases in Mr. Warner's bill that do not appear on his docket, and we have reason to believe that his official business has been conducted in a very loose and careless manner. Your committee, therefore, would refer the bill to your honorable body for such action as you may think proper for the best interests of the county.*

The report of the committee was published by the *Ypsilanti Commercial* on November 29. The same issue reported that Justice Warner had left Ypsilanti and was seen in Chicago. "We knew of his reported leaving last week," noted the *Ypsilanti Commercial*, "but wished to make certain of his departure before alluding to it. It would not be clever to have his ghost turn up in our streets after we had published that he had run away!"

TRIAL OF THE WITNESS

At about 9:00 a.m. on Friday, September 5, a man named Albert Grant, of Spring Arbor, Michigan, walked into the saloon of John Martin on the south side of Michigan Avenue. There he called for a glass of liquor, which was served to him. This glass of liquor was sold to Grant at a time of the day when such a sale was forbidden under a city ordinance.

On Wednesday, October 8, John Martin stood trial before Justice of the Peace Crane for the illegal sale of liquor on that day. Albert Grant was the principal witness against Martin. Grant, under cross-examination, explained that he was employed at two dollars a day and expenses to visit several saloons in the city and purchase drinks at each. He was then to testify at the trial.

The jury found John Martin guilty, and he was fined twenty-five dollars and costs.

That was only the beginning of the story.

On Saturday, October 8, Grant returned to Ypsilanti, this time in the custody of a deputy sheriff. This was because of a complaint made by Gerry Spear on a charge of perjury. As noted by the *Ypsilanti Commercial* of Saturday, October 18, "One clause of the declaration is as follows: 'Induced by the instigation of the devil, Albert B. Grant had maliciously and meanly swore falsely.'"

Spear was a saloon owner and partner of Myron Brown, who must have been released on bond, as he was awaiting trial for trying to burn down the Methodist church. Brown was, in fact, deputized to accompany Deputy Sheriff Fred Crouse, of Saline, to Spring Arbor to identify Grant. The warrant was issued by Justice Martillo Warner.

Mayor Snyder had been warned of the chance that Grant would be attacked on his arrival on the afternoon mail train. The mayor notified supporters of the temperance movement, and a good number were at the depot to protect Grant had the need arisen.

As Deputy Sheriff Crouse and Grant passed the saloon of George Carr on the south side of Cross Street, Carr invited the two into the saloon. Deputy Sheriff Crouse stepped just inside the door, while Grant stayed back. "The mayor told the Sheriff very emphatically that he had no business in there with the prisoner, and that he must not go in, but proceed direct to the office of the Justice. Thus the evidently cooked-up plan to get the prisoner inside was frustrated," reported the *Ypsilanti Commercial.*

When they arrived at the office of Justice Warner, it was discovered that Justice Warner had left for home just as the train arrived. He had known

Grant was on the train and would need to appear before him. To some, the absence of Warner was unaccountable, while to others it appeared to be part of a plan.

Deputy Sheriff Crouse suggested taking Grant to Ann Arbor, and he just happened to have a carriage ready. Mayor Snyder said he would go with Grant if that were the case. The account noted:

> In the mean time there was intense excitement on the stairway leading to the office, and on the walk. There were quite a number of drunken men standing around, talking loudly and swearing vociferously at the prisoner and Mayor by turns, though the special animus seemed to be directed against the Mayor. But no one dared to lay hands on him or the prisoner. They were amply prepared to protect themselves: and other parties though not spoiling for a fight, as they would not recklessly provoke a contest, yet were calmly resolved to meet the emergency, what ever it might be. The mob element would certainly have been worsted had they attempted an attack.

At this time, Prosecuting Attorney Allen arrived on the scene. The law, he pointed out, required that when the justice who issued a warrant could not be found, the prisoner was to be taken to the nearest justice. Prosecuting Attorney Allen then ordered Crouse to surrender custody of Grant to Deputy Sheriff Drake. Allen then ordered Drake to take Grant to Justice Crane. "He also very promptly and properly told the parties who were threatening violence to shut up and desist, or he would have them arrested. Counting discretion the better part of valor, they quieted down," reported the account.

Grant was taken before Justice Crane and placed under $1,000 bond, with Mayor Snyder and S.C. Hamlin acting as his sureties.

Grant appeared before Justice Warner on Monday morning, but by now the Prosecuting Attorney had been called away and could not attend. An adjournment of two weeks was requested and granted.

Grant boarded the eleven o'clock train going west. He was accompanied by the mayor and several others on hand to protect him if needed. On the same train were a number of men from several of the saloons of the city. At Ann Arbor, most of the saloon men got off the train. Two of the saloon men continued on the train to Jackson, where Grant was told that if he did not leave town that night he would be cleaned out. A warrant was sought against the two men for use of threatening language but could not be secured.

The city continued to take the liquor dealers to court, and the dealers continued to fight back. On Monday, October 20, the case was heard against William Keating. The only witness called against him was a man named Charles Clark of Napoleon, Michigan. Clark said he purchased liquor from William Keating and drank the liquor. The jury found Keating guilty, and he was fined twenty-five dollars.

The *Ypsilanti Commercial* of Saturday, October 25, noted:

> *The witness in the above case has not the appearance of a "saint," nor apparently as shrewd a man as Grant. But he can tell a straightforward story. He knows as much as the generality of those who patronize the saloons. He can tell what kind of liquor he drinks, whether it contains enough poison to intoxicate or not. We are told by a pretty stout soaker that the great trouble now-a-days is that the liquor is watered to such an extent that a witness needs to imbibe large quantities in order to tell from experience, or his feelings, that it contains a drop of alcohol.*

The following Monday, October 27, the case against Grant, after a two-week delay, came before Justice Warner. The trial did not take long. The *Ypsilanti Commercial* of Saturday, November 1, reported:

> *Gerry Spear, being brought on to the witness stand, could not swear to any personal knowledge as to the allegations in the complaint. The declaration was read to him, and he swore to it and signed it. The declaration positively asserts his knowledge of the things alleged; and he declared, on oath, that he knew nothing about it, that he was not even at the trial where, according to the declaration, Grant perjured himself.*

To this, Justice Warner said, "There is not evidence enough before me, not *half* enough to hold the prisoner a moment."

So ended the case against Grant.

An Arrest of Justice

On Monday, November 17, Ephram Bortle was to come before Justice Crane on a charge of violating the liquor ordinance. That day, instead, it was Justice Crane, who worked to enforce the law, who found himself standing before the bar of justice. The *Ypsilanti Commercial* of Saturday, November 22, reported:

> *Justice Crane was arrested on the complaint of William King for entering a plea of guilty on his docket, in a case in which the City Of Ypsilanti prosecuted Mr. King for keeping a house for the resort of persons of evil repute. The facts of the case are these: Some of the neighbors of Mr. King complained to the City Marshal of the character of the house, and he, in company with several others, made a raid on the premises, and found two women of doubtful reputation, under circumstances that justified him in taking the whole party to the lock-up. The next morning they were taken before Justice Crane, and as the evidence of their guilt was clear, Mr. King did not wish to have the case tried; so he sent his Attorney to see what penalty would be inflicted upon them. Justice Crane said he would fine them ten dollars each, and costs. The terms were very cheerfully accepted by Mr. King, and he sent his Attorney to pay the fine. He is now endeavoring to collect damages from the Justice, as he asserts, he did not plead guilty to the charge.*

That morning, Deputy Sheriff G.W. Brown of Ann Arbor stood waiting on the stairs to intercept Justice Crane before he could enter his office. Should Justice Crane fail to arrive at his office, then the case against Bortle would be dropped.

Deputy Sheriff Brown arrested Justice Crane close to his office and insisted he get in his carriage at once. Justice Crane asked Brown to let him go to his office so he could adjourn the case against Bortle. As this was not in accordance with the plans of the liquor dealers, Brown took Justice Crane by the arm and tried to prevent Crane from going to his office.

Justice Crane told Brown, "It would not pay to do the dirty work for that crowd." At this, Brown allowed Justice Crane to go to his office and adjourn the case against Bortle.

At Ann Arbor, Justice Crane appeared before an elderly justice named Clark. There, Crane showed the court he knew his rights and had the backbone to stand up for them. In the end, it was King who had to pay a security for costs, and Crane was released on his own personal recognizance and without bond. The hearing for Justice Crane was set for December 8, 1873.

The next day, Tuesday, the case against Bortle came up before Justice Crane and was hotly contested. In the end, the jury returned a verdict of guilty against Bortle. Bortle was fined twenty-five dollars and costs.

A CASE OF A GIFT HORSE

The liquor dealers tried a new tactic in December 1873 to end the prosecutions of the dealers by paying a bribe to the mayor, Watson Snyder. The dealers, as reported by the *Ypsilanti Commercial* of Saturday, December 20, raised some funds to purchase a horse at auction for the price of one dollar and a quarter. Then a messenger was sent to the home of the mayor with the horse. The messenger carried with him a note from the dealers. The *Ypsilanti Commercial* published the note, as it claimed, "partly as news and partly as a literary curiosity":

> *Ypsilanti Dec. 16th 73*
> *Mr. Snider Mare of the City of Ypsilanti we the undersign present you with a fine thourbred for a Chrismas Present. Pleas receive our Complaments also A.W.H. & J.Z.*

The mayor was not at home when the messenger arrived with the horse. The ten-year-old son of the mayor received the messenger and, according to the account, told him to "get."

The plot to bribe the mayor had failed because of a ten-year-old boy. The fate of the horse was not reported.

END OF THE FIGHT

The battle between the supporters of temperance and the liquor dealers continued into 1874. The end came in April with the annual election of the city council and mayor. The liquor dealers even tried to bring supporters into the city to vote in their favor. The tactic resulted in outrage, and the dealers lost at the polls. Mayor Snyder was returned to office, and a council was elected that supported his actions against the liquor trade.

When the new term of office began in May, the council passed new ordinances to regulate the trade of liquor. By this time, the number of liquor dealers had fallen from thirty to five. The ordinances were enforced, and the community, for the most part, seemed happy with the result.

The temperance war had ended, and the people had won.

Chapter 4
Body in the Cistern

A pleasant evening seemed in store for the family of Mrs. Elvira Barlow on Thursday, December 18, 1873, at her home on the southeast corner of Forest Avenue and North River Street in Ypsilanti. Present at the house that evening were Mrs. Barlow; her daughter Alla; Alla's husband, L.S. Whitford; a Mrs. Comer; a second daughter, May Robinson; her husband, William J. Robinson; and Mrs. Robinson's two young sons from a previous marriage.

May Robinson was up and about for the first time in weeks this evening, as she was recovering from an illness. On December 2, she had fallen ill with what the doctors diagnosed as bilious fever. This is a medical term no longer in use referring to any fever with the symptoms of nausea, vomiting, an increase in body temperature and diarrhea.

The daughter May was born thirty-three years before, when she was named Frances M. Barlow. She appears to have preferred to be called by her middle name, Mary or May. May spent the evening sitting on the floor of the parlor, watching her sister Alla play backgammon with her husband, William Robinson. Just before 9:00 p.m., May passed through the kitchen three or four times. The parlor was on the northwest corner of the house, facing Forest Avenue and River Street. On the south side of the parlor was the dining room. Adjoining the dining room on the east was the kitchen.

As May passed from the parlor once again, she was asked to take the place of her husband, William, at backgammon, as the game was finished. She said no and continued on to the kitchen. A few minutes later, her husband

William went to the kitchen for a drink of water. In the kitchen, he was surprised not to find his wife there. "Mother," he cried, "where is Mary?"

"Isn't she on the couch?" asked Mrs. Barlow

"No," answered Robinson.

"Look in the bedroom," said Mrs. Barlow.

Whitford went to the bedroom while Robinson and Alla went upstairs to look. She was not to be found in the house. Then everyone went to look outside. Mrs. Barlow went out holding a lamp. From the kitchen, there was a platform about eight feet long. At the southeast corner of the platform was a cistern about five feet deep with a diameter about the same. The curbing to the cistern was two feet in diameter, leaving an opening of twenty inches. The water in the cistern was three and a half to four feet deep. By the light of her lamp, Mrs. Barlow saw the cover to the cistern was off, with a pail of water with an undetached pole nearby. In the cistern, she saw part of May's red skirt. Mrs. Barlow shouted, "May is in the cistern."

Robinson ran up and caught hold of the skirt and drew the body along so he could take hold of the arms. Then, with the help of Mrs. Barlow and Alla, they pulled May from the cistern, head and shoulders first. A faint pulse was felt and an effort was made to resuscitate her, but with no result. The body was carried into the house. A doctor was sent for, but the heart only beat for a few minutes after he arrived.

The *Ypsilanti Commercial* of Saturday, December 27, reported:

Mrs. Robinson was a woman of more than ordinary ability—shred and smart. As the early age of sixteen, she married Wm. Stevens, whom we well knew when he was a young man, about twenty-five years ago, being then a resident of this city. From causes unknown to us, she secured a divorce from Stevens. They had two boys, now from eight to ten years old. She lived with Mrs. Elvira Barlow (her mother) for several years, sometimes, for intervals of a number of months, residing awhile at Ann Arbor, Coldwater, and a while in Ohio.

A neighbor remembered her as the "most beautiful child I ever beheld" and "smarter than a whip." She was reported to have been a writer for various eastern literary publications, including the *New York Weekly*, *The Youth's Companion* and others, under the name of "Rebecca Harding Davis."

Mrs. Robinson was also said to have been a detective who had lived in constant danger. "She is reported to have been twice deliberately fired at in a hotel at Columbus, in revenge for the exposure of a band of counterfeiters; to have been suddenly confronted with deadly weapons on various occasions,

The house at 634 North River in a photograph dated 1968. This is where the body of May Robinson was found in the cistern. *Courtesy of the Ypsilanti Historical Society.*

and to have had her footsteps shadowed by a rejected suitor, whose custom it was to appear suddenly, and either attempt or threaten violence," noted the *Ypsilanti Sentinel* of December 24, 1873, in a story reprinted by the *Peninsular Courier* on January 2, 1874.

Justice Crane formed a jury for an inquest, the members of which were sworn in at the house in full view of the body. Some, if not all, of these men most likely had known May Robinson since she was a child.

At the inquest, William Robinson testified that he first met May Robinson while he was working as a clerk at the Watson House in Coldwater. "I saw her once again at Coldwater and next at Burr Oak, near the end of October, 1873. In January I came to Ann Arbor and stayed with Mrs. Stevens, and again in February and stayed two days. That was the time of the shooting," testified Robinson.

According to William Robinson, May had told him that a man named A.F. Barr had come into her room while she was staying at Ann Arbor, took Robinson's pistol from a stand and fired it at her. She caught his hand and turned the shot, so it cut a button off her dress. Robinson said he had seen this Barr and that he was a younger man than himself, about thirty years old. At this time, Robinson and May were engaged to be married. "I don't know where she got acquainted with him," said Robinson. "He was a detective she told me."

"She had no business during the last summer," said Robinson. "She wrote for pay she said, under the name of 'Rebecca Harding Davis.'"

At the inquest, it was disclosed that during the last three months of her life, May Robinson had taken out five life insurance policies for a total of $19,500. She had three policies of $5,000 each with Michigan Mutual, the New York Mutual and the Home. There was a $3,000 policy with the National of Washington and a policy of $1,500 with the Massachusetts Mutual. There was $10,000 in the names of her children, $5,000 in her own name and, after marriage, $4,500 assigned to her husband.

She had also made a will, which she had deposited with the probate office at Ann Arbor. Under the terms of the will, her mother was made executrix and her husband made guardian of the two children. "The bulk of her property, which consisted of considerable money, together with the life insurance policies, was left to her children," reported the *Detroit Free Press* of Tuesday, December 23.

The purpose of the inquest was to determine if the death was from natural causes, accident, suicide or murder. At first it was thought May Robinson had come to her death by accident. She had, it was thought, gone to the cistern to draw a pail of water. After drawing the pail of water, she reached across the opening of the cistern to pull the cover, which was on the opposite side of the opening, toward her. She lost her balance and fell head-first into the cistern.

"The cistern was almost level with the ground, and she would have had to have reached over quite a distance, being a very small, short, frail woman. Her weight could scarcely have reached ninety pounds. Falling in so suddenly, she could have uttered only a stifled cry, and the family, at least fifty feet away, in the front parlor, could not have heard her. Once in the cistern, head foremost, we challenge the stalwart man to rescue himself," noted the *Ypsilanti Commercial.*

The fact that she had insured her life so recently, and for such large amounts, caused some to wonder if her death was a suicide. Could she have sacrificed herself in order to enrich her children and husband? She was a spiritualist and had been heard to say the next world could be no worse than this. Some believed she killed herself, inspired by her religious ideas, to the benefit of her family and to change this life for one of imagined bliss. Then again, as her life was in danger from her work as a detective, the purchase of the life insurance and the preparing of the will are easily explained.

"The jury," reported the *Detroit Free Press* of Tuesday, December 23, "after deliberating fifteen hours returned as their verdict, 'that the said Mary Robinson came to her death by drowning; but in what manner or by what means she was precipitate into the water we are unable to determine from the evidence before us.'"

After the inquest was finished, a detective for the insurance companies arrived at Ypsilanti to investigate the case. This detective concluded that May Robinson was not dead but had used her skills as a detective to try to carry out a fraud against the insurance companies. The theory was that after filing the insurance policies, she used her skills at disguise to pass off the body of another as her own. Once the policies were procured, all that was needed was to obtain a corpse, dress the body in some of her garments and place it in the cistern.

The *Ypsilanti Sentinel* noted:

> *Fortunately the case is so fresh that it can be proved or disproved immediately. We have heard the names of the jury, and we think some of them must have been personally acquainted with the deceased. They were sworn at the house, in view of the body, and went the second time to reexamine the place. The occurrence took place on Thursday night; the funeral did not occur till Sunday; and during the intermediate time we have not heard but that the neighbors had full opportunity to view the corpse. The children of the deceased must have believed it was their mother, for they manifested the grief natural to such bereavement, and children are not good actors in such cases. Finally the grave can be readily opened and the truth ascertained, if the body is still there! If not, the insurance companies will have to stand their share of the suspicion of having stolen the body to save the insurance money. As the case stands, we have no doubt that the body taken from the cistern and buried Sunday was that of the person represented.*

All accounts agree that May Robinson was no ordinary woman, but she was not the woman the accounts painted. There is no evidence that she was, in fact, the detective others claimed she was. At the inquest, it was said by her mother that she had spent the day before her death writing. Yet after her death, no trace of the manuscript could be found. It is likely that there was no manuscript to be found. May Robinson was said to have been a published author, but she most likely never published anything. She clearly was not the author who was published under the name Rebecca Harding Davis. The real Rebecca Harding Davis, a noted author of her time, died in 1910 at the home of her son, Richard Harding Davis, a respected author in his own right.

No account of the case casts suspicion on the husband, William Robinson, as the possible murderer. Yet it was he who went into the kitchen after May Robinson, he who had the insurance policies in his keeping and he who said someone had tried to kill her. Today, he would be a person of interest.

May Robinson was buried in Highland Cemetery, where her grave is marked by a headstone. On the headstone is engraved her name: Frances M. Stevens.

Chapter 5

A Serenade for Editor Pattison

The southeast corner of North Huron and West Cross Street is a vacant lot with a view of the river. This is an empty place where, for the most part, nothing seems to happen. Yet once, this now vacant lot was the focus of national attention. Here was the house and printing office of Charles R. Pattison, the editor of the *Ypsilanti Commercial.*

Editor Pattison was a man of strong opinions who did not hesitate to express his views on the subjects on which he held the firmest beliefs. He was an early supporter of the right for women to vote, and Pattison was a firm supporter of the prohibition movement. Pattison often used the pages of the *Ypsilanti Commercial* as a platform for his views on prohibition. He was a strong supporter of the Prohibitionist Party and rallied to the cause in every election.

The election of 1886 was no different, and Pattison made violent attacks in his newspaper against the Republican candidate for U.S. Congress, Captain Allen. When the votes were counted, Allen had won the election. For the Republicans, this was cause for celebration. A ratification rally was held in the roller-skating rink, now the site of the park next to the Ypsilanti District Library.

After the rally, a large bonfire was made on the corner of Huron and Michigan Avenues. Some of those who were in attendance took up tin horns, tin pans and other objects with which to make noise. Among those who were treated to this symphony of racket was Editor Pattison, who was visited just before 11:00 p.m. The visitors did not enter the yard and, after making sleep impossible for a short time, went away. Soon after, a second group appeared, and accounts of this visit differ notably.

Harvey Colburn, in *The Story of Ypsilanti*, published in 1923, gave one account:

> *The affair was staged after nightfall, with a tremendous racket. Pattison, who was entirely lacking in a sense of humor and keenly aware of the violence of his attacks upon Allen, was intensely disturbed. Although the boys endeavored to avoid damage to the house and shrubbery, a basement window was somehow broken in the course of the proceedings. Pattison appeared and shrieked his protests, but could not be heard amid the din. The crowd, however, soon dispersed. The next day, hearing of the broken window, a delegation of the boys called on Pattison and apologized for the damage. But the irate editor could not be pacified and abused them roundly. He then telegraphed over the country the report that he had been mobbed on account of his temperance convictions and took the pose of a martyr. The papers were filled with accounts of the riot in Ypsilanti.*

According to Pattison, the mob came back a second time. This time, the crowd gave three cheers for the Republican Party. Three cheers for Allen. Three groans for the Prohibition Party. Three groans for the Democratic Party. Three groans for Pattison.

Editor Pattison was a man who could express himself and did so in the *Ypsilanti Commercial* of Friday, November 5, 1886:

> *This time they came clearly with evil intentions. Marching up the walk, stamping their feet, they mounted the stoop and commenced pounding on the house, at the same time others commenced to pelt the house with stones and pans, smashing in his bay and front windows, and between the horn music, shouting, yelling and hooting, we never saw such a disgraceful affair in our city, and hope it will never be repeated.*
>
> *The smashing in the windows was well begun when his two sons and self sprang to the rescue. The crowd had fled, proceeding to Capt. Allen's residence, and gave three cheers.*
>
> *We do not charge the disgraceful mob violence of Wednesday evening upon the respectable element of the Republican Party, though the parties who entered our premises count themselves among the respectable class, and were Republicans. Of course it was the baser sort in the crowd who raided the house, and the former must bear the blame of being in bad company. The spirit of intolerance manifested by the better class has given inspiration*

The house at 314 North Huron, in a photograph dated 1944, where Editor Charles Pattison said he faced off the mob. *Courtesy of the Ypsilanti Historical Society.*

to these overt acts on the part of the bad element. The Republican sheet of this city has been of an incendiary character for months. They were not boys who were engaged in this business but those who call themselves men.

Pattison did not stop here but addressed himself to what he considered the falsehoods published by other newspapers, such as the *Evening Journal* and the *Detroit News*. The accounts published in these newspapers claimed the acts were carried out by boys, only one pane of glass was broken in the house and damages were paid liberally. Pattison wrote:

As to the boys, there might have been boys in the outskirts, but in the yard, to the certain knowledge of several members of the family, they were in stature, men, but in acts, boys. Those cheers and groans were never given by boys. One party that struck at the windows was evidently a man full grown. Another who attempted to tear down the stoop was a pretty big boy.

Single pane of glass. A glass in the parlor front was smashed in. A large bay window was broken and another cracked, and ornaments torn from the stoop. The havoc was being carried on vigorously until stopped by fear of exposure, the crowd filling the front yard either taking a part in the battery of the house, or acquiescing witnesses.

Apology, paid liberally, etc. Some party in the morning found under a brick in the yard an envelope with a note of apology and profession of *repentance and 72 cents enclosed. No names signed. It was not the note of boys, but of older heads. The money and note are in the hands of an officer. The Commercial Printing Co. had posted circulars offering $25 reward for detection and conviction of the perpetrators. We shall spend all the money necessary to bring the guilty parties to justice.*

Life went on, and soon the serenade of Editor Pattison was all but forgotten. Pattison continued to publish the *Ypsilanti Commercial* and some years later sold the paper and his house and moved away. The house and two other structures on the southeast corner of North Huron and West Cross were purchased by the City of Ypsilanti in 1970 and razed in 1971.

Chapter 6

Ypsilanti Excited

B urglars entered the store of Bowdish & Matteson on State Street in Ann Arbor on the night of February 17, 1894. They gained access by prying open a basement door in the rear of the building. Then the burglars worked the lock and made their way into the store. Once in the store, the burglars exercised good judgment as they selected silk handkerchiefs, patent leather shoes, kid gloves, jewelry, silk umbrellas and the most expensive ties. The value of the goods stolen was about $500.

After they had finished their work at the store, the burglars made their way to the barn of J.H. Nickels. At the barn, the burglars helped themselves to a horse and sleigh and carried their plunder off.

Mr. Nickels discovered the theft of his horse and sleigh at about 9:00 a.m. on Sunday, February 18. The *Ann Arbor Register* of Thursday, February 22, reported:

> *He at once traced the same to Bowdish & Matteson's store where he saw what had been done there. Having notified the officers he proceeded to follow the track of his horse and cutter and did not loose the trail until near the water tower at Ypsilanti. About this time he noticed the cutter near the barn of a farmer living a little this side. Upon inquiry, he ascertained that the farmer had found the horse near his barn early that morning and had unhitched him and put him in the barn and fed him. The horse had every appearance of having been given a hard drive.*

Officers followed the tracks of the horse and cutter in the snow to the home of Charles Simpson at 219 Prospect Street. Simpson lived here with his wife, his stepdaughter Eva and three stepsons, Tom, Bill and Irving Jones. The three Jones brothers had an unsavory reputation.

The officers procured a search warrant from Justice Beach and returned to the house on Monday morning. Washtenaw County sheriff Michael Brennan approached the house, accompanied by Deputy Sheriffs Peterson of Ann Arbor and Smith and Root of Ypsilanti, late in the morning of Monday, February 19. As they neared the house, they saw Tom Jones run out of the house and start across the lots toward the depot.

"There he goes," said Sheriff Brennan.

Deputy Sheriff Peterson started after Jones. As Peterson gained ground on him, Jones suddenly turned around and pointed a revolver at him. Jones ordered Peterson to stop. Peterson gradually walked up to Jones, his hand upraised to warn Jones not to shoot. Jones pulled the trigger, the ball striking Peterson in the left thumb. Peterson closed in on Jones and grappled with him. Peterson, assisted by John Thumb, who happened to be passing by, disarmed Jones. Sheriff Brennan, who was attracted by the shot, arrived to take charge of the prisoner.

"Jones was searched at the lockup," reported the *Washtenaw Evening Times* of Monday, February 19, "and several articles of small jewelry, such as cuff buttons, shirt studs, etc. were found. He was nervy and protested his innocence although when questioned why he carried a gun and ran away without anyone saying a word to him all that he could say was that he knew he would get the worst of it if the officers arrested him."

Peterson was taken to Dr. Edward Batwell, where his hand was dressed.

Deputy Sheriff Smith was left to stand watch at the house alone. As Smith stood watch, he saw Bill Jones leave the house and innocently saunter down Prospect Street.

Smith stepped up beside Jones and said, "I guess I'll go along with you."

The two walked down Prospect Street toward the railroad, when Jones suddenly stepped back and drew a revolver. At the same time, Jones commanded Smith to go. As Smith was unarmed, he turned to walk away. Jones then pulled the trigger to the revolver and fired three times at Smith. One shot struck Smith in the center of his back, and a second hit him in the right shoulder. Smith was lucky, as his clothing and overcoat provided protection from the shots. The bullet that struck him in the back inflicted only a flesh wound, and the one to the shoulder passed through his clothing without entering the flesh. Smith was able to walk uptown unaccompanied.

"Jones took advantage of the opportunity," reported the *Washtenaw Evening Times*, "and when last seen was going eastward on Cross St. and running in as speedy a manner as possible."

A woman who lived near the house asked what the trouble was all about. When told, she informed officers she had seen a trunk removed from the house a short time before the officers had arrived. The trunk was found at the American Express office, consigned to an Ed Smith, 435 Clark Street "Rear," Chicago. When the trunk was opened that afternoon, it was found to contain silk underwear, fine shoes, silk handkerchiefs and other articles stolen from Bowdish & Matteson's. Ed Smith had formerly lived in Ann Arbor and was evidently a friend of the Jones brothers. Smith, officers concluded, was to receive and dispose of the goods.

When the house was searched, officers found a quantity of hams stolen from Duesbiber's market. The officers also found a large quantity of stolen property from other places, implicating the Jones brothers in a number of other robberies.

The third brother, Irving Jones, was arrested that afternoon at about 1:00 p.m. When searched, he was found to have several articles of jewelry, including cuff buttons.

That afternoon, search parties went out in all directions, every man armed with a Winchester rifle. Sheriff Brennan went all over the city to borrow the Winchesters, and when one was found, two men were sent out in a rig in hopes of capturing Bill Jones. All the neighboring towns were notified and a description of him sent out. Later, when notes were compared, it seemed as if Bill Jones had been seen in forty different places, many of these miles apart.

Bill Jones, it seems, was still in Ypsilanti, as he was seen at 5:00 p.m. by William A. Burt going back into the house on Prospect Street. It was assumed he went there to get better armed, as he was known to own two heavy revolvers. Then, because he feared the officers would return to search the house, he hid himself behind a fence until dark. At 6:00 p.m., he was seen hiding behind the fence by a newspaper carrier named Tenny, who knew him well.

Nothing more was heard of Bill Jones until Wednesday, February 21, when at about 11:30 p.m., a rapping sound was heard at the door of the Simpson house. Mrs. Simpson opened the door to find her son Bill Jones standing in front of her.

"Let me in," said Jones to his mother, "and get warm."

He entered the house, approached the fire and took his shoes off. His feet were frozen, as he evidently had been exposed to the cold for a long time.

"Don't you know that this is no place for you?" asked his mother. "The police are hot after you and you should get out."

"I know that," answered Jones. "But I must get warm, I won't bother you long. Go to bed."

Jones asked his sister Eva to get him a basin of cold water. Eva got the basin and something for him to eat. He was in great pain from his feet.

After he had been in the house for about an hour, Bill Jones asked Eva for some paper. He wrote a letter to a friend in Buffalo, New York, and asked Eva to mail it for him. Then he wrote a second letter, and when done, he put it in his pocket. He then went to the side of the stove where his mother was and, crying, put his arms around her neck and asked for her forgiveness. She forgave him. Then he went to his sister and asked for her forgiveness. She forgave him.

Jones put his socks on and started for the door. Except for his socks, he was barefoot.

"Where are you going?" asked his mother.

He replied, "Oh, just out for a minute."

Four or five minutes later, the sound of a gunshot was heard.

Charles Simpson went out to see what had happened. In an orchard across the lane from the house, he found his stepson Bill Jones in a doubled-up condition, his face down in the snow and an American Bulldog revolver under the body. He had committed suicide by shooting himself in the right temple. On the body was found a note:

To whom it may concern:

This is to certify that I have this night taken my own life. My mother has closed her doors on me. My feet are frozen so bad I can't walk, so every avenue of escape is cut off. I hope the courts will not hold my dear mother responsible for anything that was found in her house that was stolen. I know she was asleep when it was brought in the house. I also wish to take all blame off Charles Simpson. He is innocent. He knew nothing about any of the things that was found. He was also asleep when they came in. I will now explain the whole thing in which I was connected. I cannot remember the night we took the hams and bacon, but they were left in the woodshed until the morning the officers came to arrest us, then they were brought in the cellar, as I expected to go to Chicago that day, but I am no nearer to Chicago now than I was then. I hope my dear mother, sister and stepfather will forgive me for the awful disgrace that I have brought upon them. I shot the officer three or four times, but I have suffered ten the pain he has. I know my mother says I cannot stay in her house so I have nothing to do but die.

My last request is, the court see that my mother has my trunk and the things which belong to me, as nothing in there was stolen except the new stuff. I think I would have made a poor burglar had I lived to try my luck. Goodbye to the world.

W.R. Jones.

After the shooting of the officer, it seems Jones had made his way to Jackson, Michigan, and then returned to Ypsilanti on a freight train. He was most likely exposed to the cold winter air all the way. The day after Jones killed himself, his mother received a letter mailed by him from Jackson. He had written:

Jackson, February 19, 1894
My Own Dear Mother,—I beg you to forgive me for the terrible disgrace that I have brought upon your house. I know you did not suspect there was anything stolen in your house or you would have made us move it right away. I know the people will look down upon you and think you knew all about it, but you was asleep when that stuff came into your house. Please do not worry over us boys, for I think we are not worthy of so good a mother. It was despondency that drove me to do it. I have been out of work so long without money or clothes so what could I do? I am in a barn, but they have searched for me, but was not game enough to go all the way. I am never coming to Ypsilanti again and I may be a murderer. There was a policeman tried to take me to the lockup and I shot him two or three times. I don't know how bad I hurt him or anything about it, but I will not stop to find out. Kiss little sister for me. Love to you and Charlie. I remain, your son,
W.R. Jones
    Don't write. I may be in the other world when you hear from me again.

The inquest was held on the morning of Friday, February 23. Dr. Batwell testified that William Jones must have died instantaneously from the shot he fired into his head. Mrs. Simpson, the *Washtenaw Evening Times* of that day noted, "exhibited some out ward feelings in her narrative, especially in relating how her wayward son had sought her forgiveness."

Eva Jones, the sister, was the third and last witness. She recounted the events of the evening when Jones returned home and killed himself.

The jury returned a verdict that William Jones had come to his "death from a pistol shot fired by his own hands."

In March 1894, Tom Jones stood trial for shooting Deputy Peterson, under the charge of assault with intent to kill. He was sentenced to the state prison at Jackson for twenty years, which was commuted to ten years. At Jackson, Jones was a model prisoner, and good time reduced the term to seven and a half years. He was released from prison in October 1901.

This event was noted by the *Ann Arbor Daily Argus* of Thursday, October 3, 1901:

> *Jones always deeply regretted the deed and after being confined in the prison he wrote a letter to Mr. Peterson expressing these feelings. He has learned a severe lesson and after his release from Jackson he lost no time in calling upon the judge who sentenced him to express his determination of being a good citizen the rest of his life. He has a job in Cleveland awaiting him and he will make a fresh start.*

Chapter 7

A Woman Saved by Her Corset

A ll seemed quiet and peaceful in downtown Ypsilanti on the evening of Sunday, October 2, 1898. Then, at 8:15 p.m., the quiet was broken by the sound of a gunshot followed by a woman's scream. Thomas Ninde had just tried to murder Mildred Young.

Thomas Ninde was a member of a prominent family, the son of the late Judge Ninde; a nephew of William Crane of the law firm of Vail & Crane, of Detroit, and of Albert Crane of the law firm of Uhl & Crane, of Grand Rapids; and a cousin of Bishop W.X. Ninde. Young Tom Ninde never showed the ambition or the ability of his family but seemed happy to make his living as a jockey and horse trainer. "Only a short time ago he was severely hurt in a runaway, and this may have had something to do with his recent strange actions," noted the *Ypsilantian* of Thursday, October 6. He was employed at the stable of the Hawkins House Hotel. It was at the Hawkins House that he met Mildred Young, who was employed there as a waitress.

Mildred Young, who had brown eyes and hair, was said to be a most worthy young woman with an unblemished reputation. At first she put up with Tom because she felt sorry for the man, as he clearly knew he was making a failure of his life and had no standing in the community. She urged him to quit drinking and be more like his father, the late judge. At this, he would cry. He admitted to her he had an ungovernable temper. The two never went anywhere together, and often Tom would walk down the street with Mildred and her sister. Sometimes Tom would chance upon Mildred when she was alone. Tom would begin a conversation with her by saying, "It

The Hawkins House Hotel, where Mildred Young was employed as a waitress and met Thomas Ninde. *Courtesy of the Ypsilanti Historical Society.*

certainly can't do any harm to talk to me." When he made his interest more marked, she refused to have anything more to do with him.

"There is one thing I will say for him, though, and that is that he was always entirely respectful in my presence and in every way a perfect gentleman," said Mildred Young.

She had not spoken to Tom for some weeks when, on the evening of Sunday, October 2, she left the Hawkins House with her sister and Mr. and Mrs. Curtis, the bartender and his wife, who was employed in the dining room. Mildred and her sister had terminated their contracts with the Hawkins House and were to leave Ypsilanti for their home in Carleton the next day.

Tom saw them and stopped Mildred directly across the street from the Cleary Business College building.

"Millie," said Ninde, "I want to speak with you a minute."

"What is it?"

"I want to speak with you privately."

"If you have anything to say to me, Tom, you can say it before this lady. You have created two scenes for me already and you must not create a third."

Mrs. Curtis could see trouble was brewing and took Mildred by the arm, as if to lead her away.

As she was doing this, Ninde quickly drew a revolver, a .38-caliber Smith & Wesson, and said, as he pulled the trigger, "Well, here is the third scene then."

Ninde shot Mildred Young across the street from the Cleary College building. *Courtesy of the Ypsilanti Historical Society.*

After shooting Mildred Young, Thomas Ninde ran to the city jail on Cross Street, to the far left of the photograph. *Courtesy of the Ypsilanti Historical Society.*

51

The shot was aimed at Mildred's heart and would have been fatal but the bullet was deflected by the steel in her corset and then buried itself in her breast. The wound was not too painful, and with assistance, she was able to walk back to the hotel. A doctor was summoned, and everything possible was done to make her comfortable.

As soon as Ninde had fired the shot, he turned to run to the city jail on Cross Street and burst in on the jailer, George Jackson, shouting, "I have done it. Lock me up."

At first, Jackson thought he was dealing with a madman, but after a few minutes, he came to understand the true state of affairs. Jackson locked Ninde in a cell and then left to learn the facts of what had happened. When he returned, Jackson found Ninde sleeping as peacefully as a baby.

The next day, Ninde waived examination in the justice court and was bound over to the circuit court for trial. Ninde was said to have looked five years older, with his mouth drawn and set, and his face frequently twitched. He said he was thankful Mildred was not dead. Ninde was then taken to the county jail in Ann Arbor by Deputy Warner.

"It is expected that the members of the family will bring all their talent and influence to bear in order to clear as far as possible the family name," noted the *Evening Times* of Tuesday, October 4.

The family may very well have used their talent and influence, as the case never came to trial. Thomas Ninde was released from jail and moved to Detroit, where he lived for the rest of his life. When he died in 1925, his obituary made no mention of his previous notoriety.

Mildred Young recovered from her wound and most likely returned with her sister to their home in Carleton. She may have carried the bullet in her breast for the rest of her life, an unpleasant souvenir of her time in Ypsilanti.

Chapter 8
Deaths of Cox and Camp

On the afternoon of Wednesday, October 25, 1905, two cousins, Gordon and Clifford Teall, were returning home from a day spent hunting. When the two were in a cornfield near the creamery at Race and Spring Streets, they made an unpleasant discovery. Resting on a fallen shock of cornstalks was the body of a young woman. She lay full length on the shock, her blue hat turned to one side, and her clothing, a blue skirt and white waist, was in perfect order as if she had lain down to sleep. The expression on her face was peaceful, and her arms were crossed over her breast. On her lips and cheek were the burns of acid. Next to the body was a bottle of carbolic acid that bore the name of "Meloche Bros., of Monroe."

Near the body of the woman, the two found the body of a man. He was on his left side, his arms and legs drawn up as if he died in great pain. The expression on his face was one of agony. He appeared to be about thirty-five years of age, wearing a white flannel shirt, a gray suit, patent leather shoes and a black soft felt hat. There were no marks on the face of the man.

The two young boys ran to the creamery, where they told the men of their discovery. At least two of the men, Seth A. Wiard and Perry Walker, went to view the bodies. The two men thought the body of the woman had been placed on the shock after death.

Wiard called Dr. James Drury, who arrived and saw the bodies in the cornfield. When he saw the body of the woman, his first impression was of suicide. He then went to the body of the man, who looked to him as if he had died in great pain.

The bodies of Cox and Camp were found near the Ypsilanti Dairy. *Courtesy of the Ypsilanti Historical Society.*

Atwood McAndrew of Mack & Mack was called to care for the bodies. He picked up hats, a handkerchief and the bottle. He noted that the cork had been replaced in the bottle after it had been emptied. McAndrew thought it possible the woman had died as she was found. No acid had spilled onto her waist, coat or neck.

The body of the man was most likely identified at the undertaking rooms of Mack & Mack as that of William Cox, a former resident of Ypsilanti. Cox was known to visit Ypsilanti often, as he liked to go fishing on the Huron River. The identity of Cox was most likely made from seven letters found on his person by a search of his clothes. The letters most likely led to the identity of the woman as May Camp of Detroit. Some years before, Cox had married a local girl, Carrie Sill, and about three years before his death, they had moved to Detroit. Cox and his wife had three children, all boys. He was a printer by trade.

One of the letters Cox wrote was to his mother, in which he told her of his plans, called himself worthless and begged forgiveness: "I have tried so hard to lead an honest, straightforward life, but I couldn't do it, no matter how hard I tried. See that the dear little boys fall into proper hands. I want them to be good, honest men and happy. Be good to Carrie, for she is the truest woman in the world."

In the letter to his mother, Cox asked that he and May be buried beside each other. "This is my dying request, bury us together, even if it is only a foot underground."

A second letter was addressed to Mrs. Margaret Wilkinson, 259 Twelfth Street:

Dear Auntie: We ask you to take good care of dear, little Alvan [Mrs.
Camp's child]. *See that he falls into good hands, that he may grow to be
a brave, true and honest man. Put $300 in the Union Trust Co. for Alvan
and do as you like with the balance.*

    *May and I die loving each other and wish to be buried side by side. Please
grant this last request, we beg of you to forgive us. We are both happy now*

    *May God bless and protect you all. May you live long and be happy.
Again asking you to forgive us*

WILL
    We took morphine which I bought in Toledo, O.

Under this, in what appeared to be the handwriting of another person, was:

Please forgive.   *MAY*

Cox had also written a letter to the Detroit Typographical Union, of
which he was a member:

Dear Friends and Brothers
*I have made up my mind to take my own life. It is a cowardly thing to do,
but if you knew the circumstances you would not blame me. I have many
friends among you who will wonder how I could do such a thing. Well, to
be brief, it is the same old story of too fast a life, whisky and women. I
hope you will all take warning and lead honest and true lives and you will
never end as I have. My dying prayer will be that the Detroit Typographical
Union No. 18 will be victorious in their present heroic struggle for the
betterment of the man who toils. If you will keep up spirits, I see nothing
but success for No. 18. Hope you will all forgive me for this rash, cowardly
act, but it is the only way that I can see out of it.*
Truly yours,
WILL C. COX

In a letter to his wife, Carrie, Cox called himself a "worthless sinner,"
adding, "and it is better for you all that I be out of the way and that you
should think of me as such or forget me." He also expressed the hope that
the two would meet in heaven.

"This woman [May] was good to me," wrote Cox to his wife. "Not so good as you, though, Carrie. You were the best to me, but I could not live loving you both, and I could not live a double life longer, so this way is best."

The next morning, Ypsilanti police officer Tom Ryan visited the site where the bodies were found. There he uncovered a second bottle that had contained carbolic acid.

Washtenaw County coroner Burchfield held the opinion that the circumstances were sufficiently suspicious to warrant an investigation. The stains of carbolic acid on Camp's face and neck seemed to indicate a struggle, but there was no evidence of a struggle at the site where the bodies were found.

"I am trying to find out," said Burchfield, "if the woman was intoxicated. If she was, it would be possible for Cox to have given her the poison before she realized what he was doing, and in that event she would not have been able to do much struggling. Cox was drunk, according to the testimony of Ypsilanti people, and now I am trying to find out if the woman was in the same condition."

What was discovered by the investigation was that May Camp was nineteen years of age. At the age of sixteen, she had run away from home and married. What became of her husband is not known, as the two had gone their separate ways. She was not divorced at the time of her death. May Camp had left her home in Detroit on Monday, saying she was going to Ypsilanti. She purchased an ounce of carbolic acid from a J.E. McAllister, a clerk in Spalsbury drugstore. He later said she was alone and acted in an ordinary way. She had purchased enough carbolic acid to kill two people.

Cox had been in Ypsilanti since Sunday and was said to have been drinking. He met a number of people he knew and asked them for money, as he said he did not have enough to return to Detroit. The couple spent Monday night at the Ypsilanti House, where Cox was not known, registering as Mr. and Mrs. Camp. The two left the Ypsilanti House and were never seen alive again.

"All last evening and this morning a curious crowd of idle, morbid people thronged the rooms of Mack & Mack's store, eager for a sight of the two unfortunates and eager for each revolting detail. In many cases, where these were wanting they were supplied by the crowd and passed on with evident relish," reported the *Ypsilanti Daily Press* of October 26.

The wife and mother of Cox arrived at Ypsilanti on the late train of October 25, the day the bodies were found. They refused to say anything except that they knew nothing of Mrs. Camp and had never seen her.

Ypsilanti chief of police Milo Gage (seated in the center) oversaw the investigation of the deaths of Cox and Camp. *Courtesy of the Ypsilanti Historical Society.*

Mr. Chester Wilkinson, the adopted father of May Camp, arrived at Ypsilanti on the 12:45 p.m. train on October 26, the day after the bodies were found. "Mr. Wilkinson is a pleasant appearing man, who made a good impression on all whom he met by his evident desire to do the right thing," noted the *Ypsilanti Daily Press* of October 26.

"May was but 19," said Mr. Wilkinson, "and was married at the age of 16 years." He said she was not divorced. Her husband had left her some time before.

"She left home Monday afternoon," he said. "No, I did not know that she had been either to Toledo or Monroe, where one of the bottles came from."

Wilkinson went to Ann Arbor and met with Coroner Burchfield, who showed him a letter believed to have been written by Mrs. Camp while in Toledo.

"No part of those letters was written by my niece and adopted daughter, May Camp. Even the three words at the end did not in any way resemble her handwriting and I believe that to have been a clever forgery on Cox's part. Neither do I believe that my niece took her own life. I believe that murder was committed."

At this time, the family of May Camp agreed she went to the cornfield with Cox to commit suicide, but they said she weakened at the last moment and Cox forced her to drink the poison. They pointed out that her face was badly burned, so, they reasoned, she must have offered resistance. There was no evidence of a hand-to-hand struggle.

Mrs. Camp had a $1,000 policy with the Prudential Life Insurance Company. This policy would be paid if Mrs. Camp was murdered but not if her death was determined to have been a suicide.

When the bodies were found, the total amount of money found on their persons was four cents. There were three pennies in the pocketbook of May Camp and one in his.

Will Cox and May Camp were not buried side by side, as expressed in the note left behind by Cox. Mr. Wilkinson arranged for Camp's body to be moved to Detroit for burial there.

The funeral of Cox was held at the Starkweather Chapel in Highland Cemetery on the afternoon of Friday, October 27. "Only the relatives were present," reported the *Ann Arbor Daily Argus* of Saturday, October 28. "There were no morbid or idle curiosity seekers present. The family were left alone with their dead, whom they buried in the family burial lot at Highland cemetery, overlooking the river where he had spent many pleasant hours."

The inquest was held on the evening of Friday, November 3, 1905, and eleven witnesses were called to testify. A man named Kirkans, who had roomed with Cox in Toledo, was called as a witness. He told the jury that Cox had informed him his wife was coming to visit and asked whether, as Kirkans would be away, his wife could stay with him. Kirkans agreed, and Cox later admitted to him that the woman coming to stay was not his wife. When Kirkans returned, Cox was gone. In the rooms, he found a scrap of paper on which was written, "Dear Auntie and Baby." Then a line about them being surprised at not hearing from her. At this, the letter ended.

When asked about the letter, Mr. Wilkinson said, "That's not her writing any more that it is mine."

"Gentlemen of the jury," said Burchfield, "stake my life that this is the writing of Mrs. May Camp."

The *Ypsilanti Daily Press* of Saturday, November 4, noted, "A pathetic feature of the inquest was the fact that while the damaging evidence was being introduced in the case the infant, fatherless babe of Cox was cooing and lisping in its mother's arms in the room, unconscious of the scene being enacted around him."

The *Detroit News* of the same date noted another feature of the inquest: that Washtenaw County prosecuting attorney Andrew J. Sawyer Jr. seemed an unwelcome guest at the proceedings. "He was satisfied that no crime had been committed. He brought out the fact that Mrs. Camp bought carbolic acid in a bottle which was found on the scene of the double tragedy. More than once, the coroner 'butted' when Sawyer was examining the witnesses. 'I have the witness and if you want to testify take the stand,' insisted the prosecutor sharply."

The inquest was called "farcical" by the *Detroit News* because Coroner Burchfield sincerely believed May Camp was murdered and made no effort to hide his opinion from the jury. Burchfield had placed on the jury Tom Ryan, an officer of the Ypsilanti Police Department, who was of the same opinion.

At the end of the proceedings, Sawyer asked the jury to think before branding Cox a murderer and bringing the stain of such a sin on his wife and children. "Remember that Cox has a family and do not brand their father as a murderer unless you have positive proof of his guilt." He called the theory of murder an idle dream.

The jury returned a verdict: "We find that William Cox came to his death on the night of October 24 by his own hand by taking a poisonous drug. We find that Mrs. May Camp came to her death on the night of October 24 by hands unknown."

Afterward, Sawyer said, "You can say that I think it's the worst verdict ever rendered by a coroner's jury in this county. Patrolman Ryan had no legal right to serve as a juror."

Later, Ypsilanti chief of police Milo Gage was asked why he allowed Ryan to serve on the jury. Chief Gage replied, "Well, the coroner subpoenaed him."

Chapter 9
Bad Start to 1909

The new year is a time of joy and celebration, a time for parties filled with singing and joy. The past is behind, and the future is open to wonderful possibilities. At least, that is the way it is supposed to be, if only for one night. The year of 1909 got off to a bad start for the Klaviter family of Ypsilanti. The old year ended with celebration, and the new year began with tragedy.

Trouble had been brewing for the family of Adolph and Emma Klaviter for some time. Adolph and Emma were born in Posen, Germany, where they had married and had three children: Richard, Ernest and Hattie. The family had immigrated to the United States in about 1900 and had settled in Ypsilanti. They were said to be hardworking Germans, and each had worked to save for a home at 222 Lincoln Street. Adolph worked on a section crew of the Michigan Central Railroad, earning forty dollars a month. Emma took in boarders at their home, took in washing and kept the house neat. Emma was said to be a handsome woman, ambitious for her children and in every way superior to her husband. The ladies who had employed Emma spoke well of her and said she had a hard time of it because of her husband. Emma liked to go to dances and attended parties with other men, as she enjoyed a good time. She saw no harm in passing a social evening.

Adolph was said to have been a man of black moods who was jealous and abusive, with an evil temper. At one time, Emma was compelled to leave him, taking the children with her and working in another town. Adolph was repentant, so she returned to him, against the advice of her friends, who feared a return of his jealous madness.

The friends were right to be concerned, as the jealous madness returned, in part because Emma continued to go to dances and parties and enjoy social evenings without Adolph. After one such dance, Adolph received an anonymous letter asking what kind of man would let his wife attend dances without him. There was trouble in the household, and the police were often called, sometimes by Adolph and sometimes by Emma. On Christmas Eve, Adolph asked Ypsilanti police officer Pierce to come to the house, as those there were making such a disturbance that it was impossible for him to sleep. Officer Pierce arrived at the house to find Emma, her sister and the boarders playing cards. They had apparently been drinking and were in an especially jolly mood. At first the party refused to quit, but after some argument, they quieted so Adolph could get some sleep.

To celebrate the end of the old year 1908 and to welcome the new one of 1909, Emma, some of the boarders and her children—Richard, age fifteen; Ernest, age eleven; and Hattie, said to have been a womanly child of twelve—went to the party at Arbeiter Hall at South Grove and Factory Streets. Adolph stayed at the house, seemingly in a good mood, and went to bed. The party came to an end, and Emma, the children and boarders returned to the house at about 2:00 a.m. Hattie begged her mother to spend the night at her aunt's house, but Emma refused. When they arrived at the house, Adolph was awake and seemed to be in an unusually cheerful and kindly mood. The boarders, Richard and Ernest went upstairs to bed. Emma, who was afraid to go to bed with Adolph, stayed downstairs and prepared to sleep on the couch with Hattie.

Hattie awoke at about 3:00 a.m. and heard her father moving about the room. Adolph drew fresh coals over the coal fire. The result of this was to leave the room in total darkness. Hattie then fell asleep again.

Emma heard her husband creeping toward her in the darkness. She only had time to make a slight motion with her head when he struck her with a sharp knife. The knife cut into her flesh with a terrible force near the right eye, cutting through the cheek, leaving her cheek to fall over her neck. He then made three short, deep cuts on the side of her chin. Had Emma not moved her head when she did, it is likely Adolph would have severed her head from her body, as he was feeling for her throat.

Her screams awakened Hattie and the boarders upstairs. For a moment, the boarders were too frightened to come down. Hattie awoke, thinking her mother had had a bad dream, but striking the light, she found her mother bleeding terribly. Adolph was not to be seen, as he had fled.

At once, the sons and boarders called for the police and a doctor. When the doctor arrived, he found Emma had lost vast quantities of blood. He treated the wounds and at once put her under opiates.

A search by police and neighbors was started for Adolph, who had fled into the night dressed only in his overalls, a shirt and socks. No trace of him was found at first. Later that morning, a Michigan Central section gang found his body a few feet from the tracks near Prospect Street Bridge. The body was facedown, with a deep cut in the head, both legs broken and the face smashed. Adolph may have received a glancing blow from a passing train, as the train crew failed to notice anything amiss. The foreman of the section crew that found the body was Charles Walters, Adolph Klaviter's brother-in-law.

As someone who had been employed by the Michigan Central Railroad, Adolph Klaviter should have known the schedule for trains passing through Ypsilanti. For this reason, some concluded that Klaviter, believing he had murdered his wife, wanted to kill himself by stepping in front of a passing train. Then again, others suggested that he ran from the house in a panic and followed the familiar tracks while only thinking of getting away and ran into the engine. At the request of the family, the body was taken to the undertaking rooms of Wallace & Clarke's instead of being taken to the house.

Washtenaw County coroner Samuel Burchfield impaneled a jury, and an inquest was held on Wednesday, January 13, 1909. Witnesses included Hattie and Richard Klaviter, Dr. R.A. Clifford, Ypsilanti chief of police Milo Gage, Officer Pierce and Louis Kemp. The jury reached the following verdict: "That upon due investigation we find that the said Adolph Klaviter came to his death by committing suicide by stepping in front of a Michigan Central railway train between the hours of 2 and 4 o'clock in the morning on January 1, 1909."

The family continued with their lives. Emma later married for a second time. Her sons grew up and entered careers in law enforcement, Richard as a Washtenaw County sheriff deputy and Ernest as an officer of the Ypsilanti City Police Department.

Chapter 10

A Crime of Sunday Baseball

O n Sunday, July 14, 1912, the McGraw's Tigers, a pickup baseball team from Detroit, came to Ypsilanti to play the Ypsilanti team. This game was played at Reinhart Field, which had been dedicated the week before. Until this, Sunday games had been played at Prospect Park. The change of location was made because charging admission was not allowed at games played at the public parks. When games were played at the public park, a hat was passed after the game. Reinhart Field had the advantage of a canvas wall enclosing the field.

A fairly good crowd attended the game at Reinhart Field, although many who had been in the habit of attending when the fee was paid by the passing of a hat were absent from the enclosure. Those who attended paid the cost of admission of either fifteen or twenty-five cents. Those who saw the game said it was a good one, ending with a score of 3–2 for Ypsilanti. There was boasting in some circles that no one would dare interfere with their game on Sunday.

This boast was made because the day before, Ypsilanti mayor Frank Norton had warned the players not to take the field, as playing baseball on Sunday was a violation of a city ordinance. Those who played, warned Mayor Norton, would be subject to arrest. There must have been a good deal of laughter over the threat of arrest for playing baseball.

Mayor Norton most likely was not laughing when, on Monday, July 15, he ordered City Marshal Milo Gage to swear out warrants for the arrest of the team manager and such players as might be accessible who had engaged

Ypsilanti mayor Frank Norton was determined to see that the laws of the city were enforced. This determination went so far as to order the arrest of the baseball team for playing on Sunday. *Courtesy of the Ypsilanti Historical Society.*

in the game that Sunday. Mayor Norton said that so long as the law forbid baseball on Sunday and as long as his office required the enforcement of the law of the city, there would be no baseball.

The Ypsilanti City Council, at the meeting of November 27, 1891, had passed what became known as Ordinance No. 53. Under Section One of the ordinance, "No person shall keep open his shop, warehouse, work-house, except only for works of necessity and charity, on the first day of the week commonly called Sunday, nor be present at any dancing or any public diversion, show or entertainment or take part in any sport, game or play within the limits of the city of Ypsilanti on the said first day of the week."

Under Section Two of the ordinance, no saloon, bar, billiard room, bowling alley, card room or cigar store could be kept open on Sunday. Further, under Section Two, "no person could remain in such a house, room or place, or in the buildings, yards, orchards or fields appertaining to the same drinking or spending their time idly or at play, nor shall any person be present at any public assembly, excepting meetings for religious worship or moral instruction, or concert of sacred music."

Any person found in violation of the ordinance was subject to a fine of ten dollars, together with the cost of prosecution. Those who failed to pay the fine could be imprisoned for any term not exceeding ninety days. The ordinance went into effect on December 15, 1891.

The case against Carl Stimpson, one of the men who played on the team, charged with violation of Ordinance 53, came to trial on Thursday, July 25. At the trial, Mayor Norton said he had received four complaints about the game played at Reinhart Field and a petition with twenty-one names on it. Mayor Norton said he did not know about the games played at Prospect Park. When asked where a game could be played, he answered, "Not here."

Milo Gage said he had never before been called on to enforce the ordinance in the eight years he had been the city marshal.

John Kirk was the attorney for Stimpson, and he argued that since the ordinance had never before been enforced, it was null and void. The ordinance was therefore annulled.

The prosecutor for the city was Lee Brown, who presented a stronger case than had been expected. He said to the jury:

> *As a law, it should be observed. If you have any laws you don't want to observe, then repeal them. That would be what was square and legal. Any amount of violation of that ordinance does not do away with it. The law is there and it stands out right and clear and so long as it stands it should be obeyed…I say gentlemen of the jury, that every man has a duty that he owes to the other citizens of the city and that is to see that all the laws passed by the city of Ypsilanti are held up and obeyed I think it is a duty to do this. Find out whether or not they have violated this ordinance and if they have it makes no difference how long it has been violated. Nothing makes any difference except whether this law was violated. I say to you that it is one of the rules and regulations of this city and if you are not going to brace up the officers that are trying to take care of you, then do away with the laws.*

The jury retired and, after a few minutes, returned with a verdict of "no cause for action." Justice Stadtmiller informed the jury their verdict had to be guilty or not guilty. The jury retired again and, after very little discussion, returned a verdict of "not guilty."

The verdict may have been decided before the trial even began, from the selection of the jury pool. The jury pool of eighteen was chosen by Deputy Sheriff Hipp, a man known to enjoy a game of Sunday baseball.

Some believed Hipp chose a jury pool of men he knew had no objection to Sunday games.

George Goodno was charged with playing baseball on Sunday, July 28, and the case went to trial on Friday, August 2.

The first witness called was Ypsilanti police officer Walter Pierce. Pierce, under questioning, admitted the score was 18–2.

Attorney Kirk asked Pierce, "Did you really call that a game of baseball?" Pierce conceded that some did not, while others did.

Officer Ryan was the next witness, and he established that Goodno had played baseball on the day in question. These were the only witnesses called. George Goodno did not testify in his own defense.

The jury retired and, after a few minutes, returned a verdict of not guilty.

At the Ypsilanti City Council meeting of Monday, August 5, Alderman Frank Whitman made a motion that Ordinance No. 53 be repealed and that the city rely on state law for Sunday protection. It was desired that the action have immediate effect.

"While five of the seven aldermen present wanted the ordinance repealed," reported the *Ypsilanti Daily Press* of Tuesday, August 6, "and that an ordinance that could not be enforced was worse than none at all, yet so summary an action was not decided upon after all, and the motion by Ald. E.R. Beal to refer the question to the committee on ordinances was carried."

The committee filed its report with the council at the regular meeting of Monday, August 19. The report of the committee noted the open and general violation of the ordinance and of similar ordinances throughout the state. The committee further noted that the ordinance had been passed more than twenty years before, and it was possible that public opinion had changed since its enactment and the public might favor its repeal. The report continued:

> *Your committee, however, is of the opinion that in a matter of such general public interest where the wishes of voters are not known it would be improper for this council to repeal the ordinance without first submitting the matter to the people.*
>
> *If a vote of the people is in favor of maintaining such an ordinance as Ordinance Number 53 then your committee believes that the ordinance should be put in such form as leave no question as to its validity, and the offices of the city should enforce the law. If the people vote against the ordinance it should be repealed.*

The committee then offered a resolution to place the question on the ballot in the November election. The resolution carried.

Mayor Norton said after the meeting he wished to carry out the wishes of the people of Ypsilanti, but if it was a matter between public opinion and legal requirements, then he deemed it his duty to follow legal direction until, at least, the law might be changed to suit the public desire.

On Wednesday, September 4, the police commissioners ordered the arrest of A.M. Renne, the manager of the Ypsilanti Opera House, for having the house open on Sunday, September 1. The case came to trial on Friday, September 6. Justice Stadtmiller ordered Elmer Conley to draw the jurymen.

John Kirk, attorney for Renne, said the performance was legal, as Renne had divided the proceeds with a charitable object. A total of eleven dollars had been donated to the hospital on the corner of Cross and Washington Streets. City Attorney Lee Brown pointed out that this did not fit the definition of charity and only served as an excuse for an activity on Sunday. The jury returned with a verdict of not guilty after fifteen minutes.

"It was by far the strongest case the city has put in its effort to have Ordinance 53 respected, and it is frankly stated that with the selecting of a jury left to those who at present are selecting it, the chances are slender for a conviction under this ordinance," noted the *Ypsilanti Daily Press* of Saturday, September 7.

"Regardless of what I had previously believed," said one man who was present, "if I had been sworn to give a verdict on the law and evidence, I would have had to find the defendant guilty."

The *Ypsilanti Daily Press* carried a full-page ad in favor of retaining the ordinance on Monday, November 4. The ad carried letters from community leaders from local churches and schools. "We appeal for the maintenance of those laws which make for the quiet and rest of the Sabbath Day, so essential to the best interests of true life and so important in its moral influence upon the childhood and youth of city," wrote the ministers of several local churches.

Charles McKenny, president of the Michigan State Normal College, now Eastern Michigan University, wrote a letter for the ad as well:

I have lived in cities where baseball, horse racing and similar forms of amusement and recreation were indulged in on Sunday, and my conviction is that they were injured by these practices. In continental Europe Sunday has come to be almost purely a day of recreation and pleasure. It would be a moral loss to America to have this custom prevail here.

It is easy to lower the moral standard of a city, just as it is easy for an individual to lower his moral standard. It demands a self-denying fight to maintain the moral standard of an individual or of a city. In order to attain the best we must give up that which is pretty good.

When the ballots were totaled after the election of Tuesday, November 5, the vote not to repeal Ordinance No. 53 had won by thirty-five votes.

Chapter 11
Throwing Eggs at the "Escaped Nun"

The Free Methodist Church of Ypsilanti was hosting Helen Jackson, who claimed to be an "escaped nun," on the night of Monday, March 1, 1920, and this resulted in more excitement than had been planned. She was one of several women who traveled the speaking circuit, making money while telling of her alleged experiences while living in a convent. Not everyone was interested in listening to what she had to say.

As the audience settled into their seats and waited the last few minutes for the program to begin, someone in the rear of the church opened a bottle containing polecat scent. As someone went in search of the source of the skunk smell, the one who did it quietly left the church.

The program continued and had just started when Mr. Jackson, the husband of Helen, was relating his religious experiences. Some mischievous boys threw perhaps six eggs at Helen Jackson. One of the eggs hit the pastor, Reverend W.E. Hosmer, directly on the chin. Others on the stage were spattered as well, as was the American flag just behind the speakers. Later, the Reverend Hosmer was to say, "The eggs were good eggs."

A call was made to the police and was received by Night Sergeant C.H. Cain. He sent Officer Truman Cole to the scene in a car. Officer Cole arrived about five minutes too late; the mischievous boys had left in a car. Who these mischievous boys were was never discovered.

The Reverend Hosmer did not believe the mischievous boys intended to spatter the American flag. "The church was crowded," he told the *Daily Ypsilanti Press* of Wednesday, March 3, "and those who threw the eggs from

The Free Methodist Church was at 758 Lowell Street in 1920. This is where eggs were tossed at the "escaped nun." *Courtesy of the Ypsilanti Historical Society.*

the rear over the heads of the audience couldn't see very well just what they were doing. But I think it is the duty of the proper officers as far as possible to protect us from such outrages in the future."

On the afternoon of Thursday, March 4, the Catholic Woman's Club of Ypsilanti held a meeting and condemned the action of the mischievous boys. That was not all the group had to say. Its statement was published in full by the *Daily Ypsilanti Press* of Friday, March 5: "We the Catholic woman's club of St. John's church in meeting assembled, hereby resolved that a vote of thanks be extended to the Masonic Lodge and the Odd Fellows Lodge of Ypsilanti in refusing the bogus nun, Helen Jackson, to speak in their respective halls."

The Masons, noted the *Ypsilanti Record*, had rented their hall to Helen Jackson but, after ascertaining the character of her address, had canceled the engagement. The Odd Fellows had been approached as well but had refused to let her lecture in their hall.

> *The action of these broad minded true Americans is the best evidence obtainable that the educated Protestants have no sympathy with persons trying to create religious strife.*
>
> *We condemn the action of the guilty parties, whoever they are, in disturbing the meeting Monday night in the Free Methodist church of Ypsilanti. We know, however, that these anti-Catholic lecturers often have their own followers deliberately stir up a disturbance at these meeting in order to make it appear that the Catholic Church opposes free speech.*

The statement noted that Helen Jackson had been exposed as a fake for years. Her real name was Helen Barnowska, and at the age of fifteen, in September 1895, she was committed to the House of the Good Shepherd, known as a reformatory, corresponding to the girls' reform school at Adrian. This was done by her sister, who considered Helen a woman of the streets and unmanageable. Helen was permitted to return to her sister, who was then living in Pittsburgh, in December 1897.

The *Record* continued:

> *Even after she left the reformatory the last time, in fact after she married, she and her husband called at the Detroit Home, and were most friendly. Like other insincere people on the anti-Catholic platform, she saw during the past wave of bigotry, a chance to make easy money.*
>
> *Helen now lectures in a garb which she represents as her nun's garb (of course she never was a nun). It is a facsimile of the costume worn by the peasant women and girls in Normandy. The Sisters of the Good Shepherd allow their charges to wear the garb as a uniform during the period in which they are on good conduct.*
>
> *No one who enters the reformatory under the Good Shepherd Sisters is ever permitted to become a member of their Order.*

The Catholic Woman's Club concluded its statement by noting the information concerning the background of Helen Jackson was from the book *Defamers of the Church*, thirteenth edition. The women offered a reward

St. John the Baptist Catholic Church as it appeared in 1920. *Courtesy of the Ypsilanti Historical Society.*

of $100 to anyone who could prove the statement was not true. The reward was never paid out.

Helen Jackson started a suit in the circuit court against the *Daily Ypsilanti Press* and the *Ypsilanti Record* for $25,000 each in damages. The headline of the story, "Egg Throwing Not Approved," was described in the suit as filed in papers with the county clerk as "malicious headlines, the more particularly to call attention to the readers of the paper to said false, scandalous, malicious and defamatory libel."

The *Daily Ypsilanti Press* noted in a story on the suit published on Thursday, March 18, that the headline "Egg Throwing Not Approved" did not sound particularly "malicious." Further, the *Press* noted, most of the statement by the Woman's Club was from the book *Defamers of the Church* and had been through thirteen editions without having to pay anything to Helen Jackson for defamation of character or for libel. The *Press* opined that "a circuit court jury will be a long time deciding to give Helen Jackson 'the escaped nun' a verdict for $25,000 for publishing resolutions passed by a woman's club, the substance of which was obtained from that book."

The *Ypsilanti Record* of Wednesday, April 6, 1921, reported that on the evening of the Friday previous the jury in the damage suit against the *Ypsilanti Press* had brought in a verdict of no cause for action. The suit against the *Ypsilanti Record* had been put over to the May term of the court.

Chapter 12

Smoking Scandal at the Normal

The Michigan State Board of Education appointed Charles McKenny president of the Michigan State Normal College at Ypsilanti, now Eastern Michigan University, in the summer of 1912. McKenny visited Ypsilanti and the college soon after his appointment and paid a visit to retiring president Lewis Jones. President Jones told McKenny that the biggest problem he would have would be the social life of the girls.

At this time, there were no dormitories on the campus; students lived in boardinghouses in the city. Students could only stay in boardinghouses approved by the college. The houses were segregated by gender; male and female students could not live in the same house. The boardinghouses were owned and overseen by landladies, who lived in the houses with the students they rented to. There were few, if any, absentee landlords at this time. Then again, if there was no landlord living in the house, then the house would not have been approved by the college as a place where students could live.

President McKenny chose to take action and did so soon after assuming the office of president. On the afternoon of July 27, 1912, Grace Fuller, dean of Normal women, entertained at her home a large portion of the 366 women who rented rooms to Normal students. After a short musical program by Miss Nellie Johnson, President McKenny was introduced to the women.

President McKenny spoke on the policy of the college. He said he would carry out the plans already formulated by President Jones and seek to define more clearly the agreement among students, landladies and the college. The rules the landladies now had to observe were:

Lewis Jones retired
as president of the
Michigan State Normal
College in 1912. Jones
told incoming President
Charles McKenny that
his biggest problem
would be the social life
of the girls. *Courtesy of
Eastern Michigan University
Archives, Ypsilanti, Michigan.*

*1. The college keeps an approved list of rooming and boarding places. It
desires to put on this list all homes that will cooperate with it in furthering
the welfare of its students. Young women who desire to engage rooms in
houses not on the approved list will consult the Dean of Women.*

*2. Students are expected to stay the full term in the room first engaged
unless good reasons can be given for making a change. Such change can be
made by the women students only after consultation with and approval of
the Dean.*

*3. Women students cannot engage rooms where there are men (single or
married) roomers.*

4. Students may expect the following accommodations:

    *a. Usual bedroom furniture; also table, chair (3), waste basket,
bookcase, closet space.*

    b. Change of bed linen every week. The rest of the bedding should be clean.

c. A thorough cleaning of the room each week by the landlady, unless other arrangements are made.

d. Bath privileges.

e. Reasonable parlor privileges.

f. Suitable light for evening work.

g. Adequate heat for comfort.

5. *A room proper in its appointments for receiving callers should be accessible to our women students in houses in which they room. Under no circumstances should callers be entertained in the rooms of women students. A folding bed or sanitary couch does not transform a bedroom into a reception room.*

6. *Young women may receive callers on an average of once a week on Friday or Saturday evenings, or on Sunday. Such callers should never stay after ten o'clock.*

7. *Young women are expected to observe the rule of propriety which prescribes that they shall not go out of the city evenings accompanied by young men, automobiling, canoeing, or to entertainments unless chaperoned. Justifiable exceptions to this rule may be allowed by the Dean of Women.*

8. *Householders expecting to be away from their homes regularly during the day or during a longer period of any term should not take students into their homes. Cases of seemingly justifiable exceptions to this suggestion should first be explained at the office of the Dean of Women, if women students are expected.*

9. *Any change in the management of a house where women students room arising after a term opens should be brought to the Dean's attention before such change occurs.*

10. *Prompt report should be made to the general office of illness of students.*

11. *We feel that persons taking our students into their homes are in a measure responsible for their health and conduct. While we do not expect landladies to deal with cases that may prove troublesome or annoying, still we do expect such matters to be brought to our attention as soon as possible. Any person who shields a young woman or young man known to be conducting herself or himself contrary to the spirit of the best womanhood or manhood is knowingly contributing to conditions which may lead to the dishonorable dismissal of such student from this school and the withdrawal of the house from our list of approved places for students.*

"It is a great privilege," said President McKenny to the ladies, "for any city to have the opportunity to influence humanity as Ypsilanti is doing

Charles McKenny moved quickly
to set in place the rules for the girls
and overcame the opposition of the
landladies. *Courtesy of Eastern Michigan
University Archives, Ypsilanti, Michigan.*

Grace Fuller was the dean of women at
the Normal College in 1912. She worked
with President McKenny to enforce the
new rules for the girls. *Courtesy of Eastern
Michigan University Archives, Ypsilanti,
Michigan.*

through the nearly 3,000 teachers who annually are enrolled at the Normal College. In the absence of a dormitory system the home into which the students go are in a sense part of the institution."

"The presence in the city," continued President McKenny, "of hundreds of young women from 17 to 20 years of age puts a serious responsibility upon the homes which receive them. Each home should strive to do for the young women which it receives what the home would like to have done for its daughter, were she away from the home circle."

The ladies, in public, at least, expressed full support for most of the rules. There were two rules, however, that caused them to express some concern. The first of these rules was the one involving the use of the parlor.

"I feel I shall have no privacy in my own house," said one. "I know it is for only three nights a week, but suppose you have 12 girls and all have company. What are you going to do? I never have had girls myself who had much company, and I have always stayed with the girls a good deal. Yes, there has been too much canoeing and automobiling at night. But; so far as I am concerned, my girls have been good and nice."

"I like all the new rules and regulations except one," said a landlady who said she had kept roomers for twenty-five years. "That is the rule about the landlady's parlor. The girls always expect to serve some kind of refreshment. It means that our parlors will just have to be made over into dining rooms— that is all. I try to be good to the girls, but if you fix up a nice parlor and the girls do things there that you would not do yourself and spoil it, it is hard. I have a nice suite I rent, and I think if girls cannot be trusted, they ought to be sent home. I don't think there is much irregularity among the students."

The landladies also expressed concern over the rule requiring them to provide chaperones for the girls.

"What is one to do," asked one landlady, "if one student wants to go canoeing, and another automobiling and another wants to go out of town? She can't be everywhere at once...Besides, my students say that if any chaperones go out canoeing with them, they'll drown them. You see our very lives are in danger."

"As to chaperones," said another landlady, "how many landladies would want to risk their lives in a canoe among the stumps on the Huron or joy-riding in a speedy automobile?"

In time, everyone came to accept the changes in the rules, and peace seemed to come over the community.

As the landladies of Ypsilanti had to adjust to the changes made by President McKenny, the community and the world changed as well. The year 1912 gave way to the years of the First World War, which in turn gave way to the 1920s and the time of the flapper. The role of women changed with the times, and girls wore their hair bobbed and their skirts short and used makeup. For some, these changes seemed to show the world was getting worse. The changing styles received critical comment, criticism and condemnation.

Normal College president Charles McKenny did not share the view that the styles of young women showed the world was entering into a state of moral decay. He, instead, saw the promise of the future and defended the younger generation. "I have known modern girls for 40 years and the present generation of girls is the finest type that ever stood on the campus," said President McKenny to the Detroit Federated Women's Club on Friday, February 24, 1922. He continued:

> *Bobbed hair, short skirts and red cheeks go together. Let the girls put the skirts any length they please. The length of the skirt isn't going to affect the American girl.*
>
> *If the young men, instead of talking so much about girls and passing resolutions of disapproval as some of them are doing, would talk about the men they would do better.*
>
> *I'm here to defend the modern girl and the modern boy. I've no sympathy with this idea that is being continually harped on that this world is growing worse. It is in the process of growing better all the time.*

President McKenny was about to find himself at the center of a controversy over the social morals of the time. This began when the Normal College sent a letter to the landladies who rented rooms to students of the college at the end of the winter term of 1922.

The letter informed the landladies that seventeen women students of the Normal had been dismissed and thirteen others had been placed on probation. The college sent the letter as a way to emphasize that smoking, street flirtation and late hours among the female students would not be tolerated. The letter read:

> *You will probably realize that in so large a body of students there are some eliminations necessary each term. For instance, so far as women students are concerned, the fall term closed with nine requested to withdraw during the term or not to re-register and with fourteen on probation. This term five were obliged to withdraw under pressure due to disapprobation during the*

The Michigan State Normal College campus as it appeared in 1922. *Courtesy of the Ypsilanti Historical Society.*

term and at the end of the term 17 were requested not to re-register and a list of thirteen are now receiving notice of having been placed on probation.
The reasons for this procedure included undesirable attitude toward work, inability to do the work, class absences, as to make us unwilling to longer take responsibility, psycho-neurotic mental condition, dishonesty in word, in school work and in financial matters, and smoking. All cases were carefully investigated, student, matron and faculty testimony was secured, and many of these cases had had frequent counsel and advice and not one of the cases had less than two of the above charges against them, and some had nearly all of them.
So far as social indiscretions is concerned, we wish to call your attention in particular to the kinds of acts for which the girls were recently dismissed. The list included attentions from many and some times strange men, allowing undue familiarities from men who were casual acquaintances, sometimes from several men in one term, constant week night dates, with evasions of closing hours, auto riding without permission, and sometimes by street pick-up, all night absences from rooming houses without permission of either matrons or dean, walking in

parks and gardens at night and gaining access to rooming houses by way of windows. I am sure you will all agree with us that no normal school can retain people known to do these things.

Regarding smoking, a word should be said. The college does not enter into the discussion of the question of whether it is any worse for a woman to come in at two o'clock in the morning than it is for a man, nor whether it is any worse for a young woman to get drunk than it is for a young man. There are a good many who would contend that it is just as wrong for a man to do these things as it is for a woman. The position of the college is simply this: The taxpayers of the State of Michigan are supporting the Michigan State Normal College for the training of teachers. They have a right to say what sort of teachers they want in their schools. The college is certain that there is not a school board in Michigan that would elect as teacher a young woman who smoked cigarettes if it knew she did so. That being the case, the Normal College will not knowingly permit any young woman to remain in school, much less graduate her, who smokes tobacco, and moreover, it will consider no house a proper place for its young women to room that permits girls to smoke. Until the people of Michigan change their attitude and are willing to take women smokers as teachers the college will adhere to this policy.

So far as the social rules are concerned, the college holds the men of the college to the same standards as the women whenever college women are involved.

The letter was signed by Normal College president Charles McKenny and Bessie Leach Priddy, who in 1922 was the dean of women.

On Wednesday, April 12, the *Ypsilanti Daily Press* published a story on the dismissal of the girls from the Normal College. News of the dismissals spread far and wide and was reported by the *New York Times*.

"We are old enough to look out for our own morals," was a common expression among both the men and women of the college, noted the *New York Times* of Thursday, April 13. Then the *New York Times* of Friday, April 14, reported that the female students were "particularly peeved" at the Women's League, an organization supported by student dues, although undergraduates had little voice in its operation. The governing council of the league was made up of female members of the faculty and the "presidents" of the rooming houses.

"It was through this league," reported the account, "that Dean Priddy obtained much of the information on which charges against the seventeen

Bessie Leach Priddy was the dean of women in 1922 and was the one who sent the letter informing the landladies that seventeen young women had been expelled by the Normal for social indiscretions. *Courtesy of Eastern Michigan University Archives, Ypsilanti, Michigan.*

girls were based. This organization, the girls declare, is little short of a spy system. A close check is kept on all girls and they cannot move from one rooming house to another without the information reaching the Dean."

"That we come here to school to learn to be teachers, usually at more expense than our parents can easily bear, shows that our intentions are serious," said a young woman to the *Detroit News* on Wednesday, April 12. The young woman was identified only as the president of a prominent campus organization. "Let our work stand on its merits. Everybody is frivolous once in a while. But certainly no one as far as I know has done anything vicious or wicked or menacing. If a girl doesn't do her work she expects to be dropped. But job control for teachers on the basis of good manners and the proprieties is objectionable."

As a result of the publicity, Michigan governor Alexander Groesbeck, on the morning of Tuesday, April 18, asked Thomas E. Johnson, the state superintendent of public instruction, of the state board of education, to investigate the state of affairs at the Normal. Following this announcement, President McKenny prepared a statement outlining his position on the matter.

President McKenny began by noting he had been out of the state at an educational meeting and returned on April 16 to learn that the state and country had been flooded with the announcement of the young women being dismissed from the college. His first reaction, he wrote in a moment of righteous indignation, was to call the statement a "lie." Then, he noted, in a cooler moment, he would have said it was an "untruth." He continued:

The Normal College is maintained by the state for the training of teachers. Every one who enters the college must sign a statement that he intends to teach, consequently there is a moral obligation on the part of the faculty to eliminate from the student body students who do not give fair assurance that they can develop into satisfactory teachers. To permit students who cannot make teachers to remain would not be fair to the students themselves nor to the state. It is to be expected that out of every hundred students, coming from a great variety of homes, there would be a few, two or three, who would not have the social stability to develop in two years into the sort of teachers that Michigan wants.

It must be remembered that six or seven hundred of the young women of the college are just 17 to 18 years of age. They lack maturity, and many of them have had little social experience. It is not to be wondered at that some of them cannot sustain themselves in the atmosphere of college freedom.

McKenny noted that girls had been asked to withdraw for three main reasons:

First, for their welfare. The college is not willing to take the moral responsibility for the character of a young woman who is not willing to live up to the common sense regulations of the college. In nine cases out of ten when parents know that their daughters lack self-control they are eager to take them home.

The second reason is that girls who do not show a reasonable amount of self-control cannot be safely recommended to teaching positions. The college every year writes to superintendents that employ its recent graduates for information as to how they are getting on, and the greatest single failure that is reported is the failure of social poise and self-control.

The third reason why young women have been asked to withdraw is justice to the student. It is not fair to the young women who live proper social lives to have their good name injured by young women who violate the social proprieties, and it takes but a few of the socially indifferent to give a name to an institution. Parents who send their daughters to a state college have a right to expect that the influence of the college will be uplifting and not otherwise.

McKenny stated that no girl had been asked to withdraw unless the case was clear and defensible. He further stated that the claim that girls were discredited because of bobbed hair had no foundation. "Some of the best students on the campus have bobbed hair," he added. "The college would as soon dismiss a girl for having blue eyes as for having bobbed hair."

Then McKenny explained that of the seventeen students asked not to reregister,

> *only five were asked not to return because of violation of the social rules, and three others because of poor class work and disregard of the social rules. During the six months of the present school year about seventeen have been asked not to return because of the violation of the social rules. Against a total of seventeen asked not to return because of unsatisfactory social life stands a list of nineteen now in college on probation, whom the college is trying to save to themselves, their homes and the teaching profession.*

In conclusion, President McKenny stated that it was common knowledge that smoking among girls in high school and college was increasing. It was the opinion of the college that school boards in Michigan would not choose a teacher for their school if they knew she smoked. Since the college was to supply teachers for the schools of Michigan, it had taken the position that girls who smoked were not suitable candidates and, as a result, should not remain in the college. Four girls had been asked not to return because they smoked; three admitted they began smoking before entering high school and the fourth in her sophomore year in high school.

> *The college believes that the fathers and mothers of Michigan do not care to have their daughters go to a college that permits smoking. It may be wrong in this conclusion, but feels quite certain that it is not. The faculty of the college has but one aim—and that is to conduct the institution in such a way as to turn out the best possible teachers for Michigan schools and to create in the college such a moral, intellectual and social atmosphere the fathers and mothers of the state will not hesitate to send their sons and daughters here.*

On Tuesday, April 18, the Woman's League and the Student Council of the college unanimously passed resolutions in support of President McKenny and Dean Priddy. The next day, Wednesday, April 19, the Matrons' Association held a special meeting in Starkweather Hall, where a resolution approving the action taken by President McKenny and Dean Priddy was unanimously passed.

The state board of education held its regular monthly meeting at the Normal College on Saturday, April 29. President McKenny spoke on the seventeen students dismissed from the college as part of his report. He followed this with an oral report on each of the women dismissed from the college. The board then unanimously adopted a resolution endorsing his action.

The action of the board was intended to bring the controversy to an end. In this the action failed, as one of the seventeen students was taking the case to court.

Alice Tanton was one of the seventeen girls expelled from the Normal College. She chose to take legal action to be readmitted to the Normal College. The case came before the Washtenaw County Circuit Court on Monday, June 12, with Judge George Sample presiding. There was no jury, as the final decision would be made by Judge Sample.

Walter Nelson was the attorney for Alice Tanton. She was the first witness. "I am not an inveterate cigarette smoker," testified Alice Tanton. "I never have smoked but three times in my life. I never have done anything in my life for which I need hang my head in shame. I want more than anything else to be reinstated in the Michigan State Normal College at Ypsilanti, and, if I were reinstated, I would obey every rule to the very best of my ability."

At one point in the proceedings Alice Tanton walked to the bench and displayed her fingers and white teeth to Judge Sample.

"Do these look like those of a habitual smoker?" she asked.

Judge Sample looked down at her and, smiling, said they "look pretty nice."

Tears came to her eyes when she mentioned the death of her mother fourteen years before. She told of living with her father until about 1915 and for seven years living with her sisters Dorothy and Gladys at 2360 West Grand Boulevard in Detroit. Her father, she said, cast her off after she was expelled from the Normal, and now she had only her sisters.

She also told of automobile rides she had taken with students of the University of Michigan and her former high school principal at Rochester. Under questioning by Assistant Attorney General O.L. Smith, who represented the Normal, she was asked about one of these rides.

"Where did you sit in the coupe?"

"In the man's lap."

"And did you at any time, to keep from slipping, find it necessary to put your arms around the man's neck?"

"I did not."

Smith asked if, just for a whim, she had accepted an invitation for a ride from any man she did not know.

"I should certainly not regard any such action as a whim," she indignantly replied.

The next witness called to the stand was Normal College president Charles McKenny. He testified:

> *I had never known Alice personally before today. I have been too busy to give the case much of my personal attention before. The perfectly candid attitude she has on the stand today has impressed me greatly. I believe she has told the truth, and I want to believe in her. And, what is more, I like the girl.*
>
> *I am bound to conduct the college as the public sentiment of Michigan demands. Public opinion, I have learned from school superintendents, editorials, W.C.T.U. women and from the opinion of school men throughout the state who have told me they would not hire a girl who smoked.*
>
> *There are certain standards of conduct which the race has set up for our time, and those standards draw a fine distinction between men and women. There is no denying the fact that people draw that distinction. A man may stay out till 2 a.m. and not be questioned, but let a girl do the same thing and she is immediately questioned. The distinction is there; we must accept it.*
>
> *I am not saying it is immoral for a girl to smoke, but it is an impropriety very much censured. Smoking has a bad effect on men and women. The group that smokes, it has been determined by experts, is of lower standard than that which does not smoke. Yes, it would be fine if all people could be dissuaded from smoking.*

"Do you smoke?" McKenny was asked by Nelson.

"No."

"Ever smoked cigarettes?"

"Yes, when a senior at M.A.C., perhaps once a week."

"Did you ever have an expressed rule that students of your college should not smoke?"

"No."

"But you do object to people smoking cigarettes, do you not?"

"I have a decided personal opinion against women smoking. When I have reason to believe that a girl on the campus smokes I will dismiss her. The fact that a girl has smoked does not disqualify her from becoming a teacher if she gives up the habit and goes straight afterward. I would admit a student to college who had smoked in high school but who had quit the habit."

"In dismissing Alice Tanton from college," asked Nelson, "you inflicted the greatest punishment you possibly could upon her, did you not?"

"Well," answered McKenny, "I could shoot her, I suppose, but I wouldn't for that would hardly be legal."

Alice Tanton's attorney, Walter Nelson, began the second day of proceedings with a surprise. He had subpoenaed University of Michigan president Marion L. Burton; Joseph Bursley, dean of men; Prof. Evens Holbrook, of the law school; Dr. Rollo E. McColter, professor of anatomy; and Dean Allan S. Whitney. Nelson wanted to ask each of the faculty members called to testify to a hypothetical question about their procedure should they find a girl under their jurisdiction who was addicted to cigarette smoking. Nelson wanted to establish the fact that they were or were not averse to women smoking.

As Nelson tried to ask his question, Deputy Attorney General O.L. Smith, appearing for the Normal College, objected to every question put by Nelson. Judge Sample upheld the objection in each case. University president Burton occupied the witness stand for forty-two minutes, during which Nelson asked him forty-four questions. President Burton did not answer a single one asked. The result was to retard the proceedings by repeated legal arguments as to the admission of evidence.

That same morning, Bessie Leach Priddy, dean of women, was called to testify. She told the court of having read a report on the conduct of Miss Tanton. Mrs. Priddy said there had been one girl at the Normal who had confessed to being an inveterate smoker. This girl, continued Mrs. Priddy, had rings under her eyes, her skin was dry and her fingers were discolored. The girl, noted Mrs. Priddy, was also very nervous. From these symptoms, Mrs. Priddy judged Miss Tanton smoked.

Mrs. Priddy told of an interview she had with Miss Tanton and her older sister, at which she told the sister it would be best for her to take Miss Tanton home. She said she told the sister she was sorry Miss Tanton had fallen in with the wrong crowd. Mrs. Priddy said she told Alice Tanton she could not be reinstated at the Normal. At the end of the interview, said Mrs. Priddy, she put her hand on the shoulder of the sister and said, "Take the little girl home and look after her."

A Miss Beal, assistant to Dean Priddy, told of finding cigarettes in Miss Tanton's room and finding cigarette ashes on the floor of Miss Tanton's room around a wastebasket, as well as finding ashes in an ashtray on a table.

Two young men testified as to seeing Alice Tanton smoking with another young woman as the two sat in an automobile on Ellis Street, now Washtenaw Avenue, early in the winter term. As the two—first Frank Gordon and then Henry Johnson—testified, Alice Tanton watched them with an expression of disdain. Immediately after the two had testified, Alice Tanton took the stand to swear she had never stopped on Ellis Street in an automobile and had never smoked there.

Dean Priddy was back to the stand that afternoon, and a letter was introduced as evidence. It read:

> *Alice Tanton, aged 18, mentally 157. Accused of smoking. Bobbed hair, childish in appearance. Motherless since five years of age. Went with a wild bunch at Rochester high school. Lives with two older sisters in an apartment in Detroit. Father does not live with them. Says father is very severe with her. Accusation brought by Mrs. Moffat, a pretty young bride from DePaul University—says husband smelled smoke—windows open much. Cigar stubs in basket, gradually disappearing box of cigarettes in table drawer. Matches and ashes on carpet. Thinks her unreliable socially also. Girl claims she used cigarettes to burn edges of pictures to decorate the walls. Pictures there not highly desirable, but three have burned edges. Girl admits smoking at home. Says she learned down at Orion, also admits she and seven others in the fall term went walking one evening and smoked.*

The words "bobbed hair" had been crossed out but still could be read. In the margin of the letter were the words "must go" in President McKenny's handwriting.

Mrs. Priddy was emphatic in her denial that bobbed hair had anything to do with the dismissal of Alice Tanton from the Normal. "There is no connection in my mind between bobbed hair and cigarette smoking or in the infraction of any rule of our college. I do not know and I do not care whether the girl smoked cigarettes in a sparsely settled street or whether she smoked them down town. It is all the same to me. She smoked them, and that is what matters," said Dean Priddy.

The attorneys made their closing arguments that afternoon, and Judge Sample told the attorneys to submit their briefs within ten days. Judge Sample handed down his decision in the case late in the afternoon of Friday, September 8. He upheld the right of the Normal College authorities to enforce the rules against smoking and whatever else may be considered conduct unbecoming of a prospective teacher. He denied the petition of Alice Tanton that would have compelled the Normal College to readmit her as a student.

"I have no plans for the future," said Alice Tanton after being told of the decision. "I feel at present that there is no use in my trying to study further for the teaching profession in another college, since the record against me at Ypsilanti will always be there to prejudice school boards against me."

Her attorney announced his plans to appeal the case to the Michigan Supreme Court. The case was submitted to the Michigan Supreme Court on January 8, 1924. The case was decided by the court on March 5, 1924. The Supreme Court of Michigan upheld the decision of Judge Sample and turned down the appeal of Alice Tanton.

Chapter 13
Fracas at the Fountain

For many years, it was the practice of the graduating class of the Michigan State Normal College, now Eastern Michigan University, to present the college with a gift. This was usually a portrait of a member of the faculty or the reproduction of some great work of art. The class of 1898 chose to present the college with a fountain. The fountain consisted of a large basin within a basin, with the outer basin about twenty-five feet in diameter. The ground was banked up to the fountain with palms and flowers, with water plants growing between the inner and outer basins. The intention was to make the site of the fountain beautiful.

The *Washtenaw Evening Times* of June 6, 1898, noted:

> *But then, the fountain will come in for its share of the beauty. It will be 14 feet high and the water will shoot up a few feet more. The height of the first pan is seven feet and the second pan is three feet and seven inches higher. The diameters of these pans are five feet and eight inches, and two feet and ten inches respectively. The extension from the top pan consists of a bunch of lilies, from which flows the water. All in all, it is very beautiful and a fitting memorial.*

The fountain soon became a local landmark and served as the background for many photographs. It also saw use as part of the initiation rites of the student societies. The fountain was also a convenient place to dunk men of the University of Michigan who had the audacity to date girls of the Normal College.

The Normal Fountain was for many years part of the campus of the Michigan State Normal College, now Eastern Michigan University. *Courtesy of Eastern Michigan University Archives, Ypsilanti, Michigan.*

One university male with the audacity to date a Normal girl arrived in Ypsilanti on the evening of Tuesday, June 2, 1925, and was dunked into the fountain. The following evening, Ypsilanti was rife with rumors of a university fraternity coming over to "clean up" as an act of revenge. That evening, two cars filled with university men, one displaying a red flag, scouted through the city.

The men of the Normal College had gathered west of the Training School, at Welch Hall, at about 9:30 pm. waiting for the Ann Arbor men to appear. The plan was for the Normal College men to stand together back to back. At about 10:00 pm., the cars carrying the men from the university arrived, were driven past the gathering west of Welch and made straight for the fountain. There they tossed in all the Ypsilanti men they could find.

The *Daily Ypsilanti Press* of Thursday, June 4, reported:

> *The Ypsilanti men then, after pausing a minute while leaders frantically begged for organization, ran to the fight. Men went into the water in rapid succession from then on. Fairly sharp lines were drawn between the two camps; and any who ventured across was sure to be piled on, five to one.*
>
> *The lines were growing more and more definitely drawn, which separated Ann Arbor from Ypsi men when a Michigan man attempted to make a speech, and the fighting stopped. Registrar Steimle, who had just arrived,*

The men of the Alpha Sigma Phi fraternity in 1925, as they appeared in the 1925 *Michiganensian. Courtesy of the Bentley Historical Library, University of Michigan, from* Michiganensian, *1925.*

The Normal Fountain was near the Administration Building, now Boone Hall. *Courtesy of Eastern Michigan University Archives, Ypsilanti, Michigan.*

then called the Ypsilanti crowd to the steps of the Administration Building [now Boone Hall] *where he could make himself heard, and ordered the men to go home.*

"Michigan first," came the reply, and all stood their ground. Edwin Stahl, the president of the men's union, called on the men from the university to send over a speaker. A man named Dewey came over and said the men from Michigan had come over as they did not like what had happened the night before. The university men had come in a body, said Dewey, for protection.

"We are satisfied," said Dewey. "We have thrown in more men than you have."

At this, the men of the Normal College announced their willingness to continue the fight.

Dewey then retracted this part of his statement and called it a draw. He said if the men of the Normal College agreed, the men of the university would withdraw.

It took the crowd thirty to forty-five minutes to disperse, but it did so without further trouble.

"A large crowd of girls and townspeople watched the fighting," noted the account. "Cross Street was lined with cars."

A few of those tossed into the fountain had been injured, but none seriously. At least one was taken to a hospital for treatment.

The account reported that Robert I. Barber, an attorney from Detroit, had spoken at the chapel at the Normal College the week before. He had talked of the days when Normal men would tie up the "sheiks" from the university who came to Ypsilanti during calling hours. Barber had also spoken of the Normal men greasing the tracks of the interurban, a trolley car that ran between the cities, so the cars could not get up the hill on Cross Street and the university men had to walk back to Ann Arbor. This talk, the account noted, was credited with furnishing some of the incentive for the clash at the fountain. "Normal men are no more lacking in spirit today than formally," the account reported, "they have demonstrated quite satisfactorily, they feel."

The next evening, rumors were rife of a second confrontation between the Normal College men and the men of the university. Some two hundred Normal College students, dressed in old clothes and some carrying sandbags, had gathered on West Cross Street to repel the invaders should they appear. Registrar C.P. Steimle informed the crowd that he had made preparations for the men of the university should they come. He called on

Normal College registrar Clemens P. Steimle called for order and urged the men of the Normal and the university to go home. *Courtesy of Eastern Michigan University Archives, Ypsilanti, Michigan.*

the students to disperse, but they refused to leave.

To keep the fight away from the campus, the students were forbidden to set foot on college grounds. The college men then moved to Recreation Park at about 9:30 p.m. to await the invaders, followed by a crowd of co-eds and townspeople.

"A detachment of state police patrolled Cross Street, prepared for trouble when it should arise," reported the *Normal College News* of June 12.

At Recreation Park, a man named Ed Perry told the students he had helped them the night before and now the university men were out to "get him." At his suggestion, the students moved to the middle of the park, where they sat down to wait. As they waited, students told stories and sang songs to entertain the crowd.

"Numerous conflicting reports came in from scouts. A group of three arrived at one time to report they had seen four hundred Michigan men gathered behind the science building. Another report had a like number gathered in the woods along the river road to Ann Arbor. Other groups drove over to Ann Arbor where they reported the streets deserted, the men having all left for Ypsilanti," reported the account.

Normal College's Cough Joseph "Doc" McCulloch, who was an associate professor of physical education, arrived at Recreation Park and urged the men to parade in the streets or make a demonstration when they left the park. He then drove to the places where the Michigan men were reported to be gathering and returned to the park to tell the men there were no such gatherings in town.

The Normal College men were concerned about the possibility of the Michigan men waiting for them to break up and then pounce on the smaller

Left: Cough Joseph H. McCulloch, associate professor of physical education at the Normal College, spoke to the men of the Normal the night after the dunking. *Courtesy of the Ypsilanti Historical Society.*

Below: Normal College president Charles McKenny called the fountain episode closed. *Courtesy of Eastern Michigan University Archives, Ypsilanti, Michigan.*

Charles Oakman must have recovered from his broken knee, as he was the chairman of the Jhop, an annual dance at the university, in 1926. *Courtesy of the Bentley Historical Library, University of Michigan, from Michiganensian, 1926.*

groups. Cough "Doc" McCulloch made one last long search, taking him to Ann Arbor. On his return, he assured the Normal men there were no such groups. Then he moved the crowd back to the grandstand, where the students, including the girls, gave the Normal College yell. Then the crowd broke up and went home.

"Many townspeople and students were out at the field looking on," concluded the account. "Co-eds paid little attention to 'ten o'clock rules.'"

At the last general assembly of the term, Normal College president Charles McKenny said:

I think any body of students is justified in resenting an invasion of its campus by students from another campus. I think this would be accepted on any college campus.

The invasion was caused by a mistake on the part of students of this institution. The men admit it freely it was a mistake.

We can't afford to have any feud start between the University and the Normal College men. We have always had peace and we propose to have peace.

Then President McKenny asked: "That is right, is it not?"
To this, the students applauded.

The *Normal College News* of June 19 published a letter from University of Michigan student Charles Oakman, who had been injured on Wednesday night. The letter was addressed to the secretary of the men's union. Oakman wrote:

> *I want to express to the members of the Men's Union my deep felt appreciation for the wonderful box of roses sent to me. They were very beautiful and I enjoyed them immensely as did everyone who came into my room.*
>
> *With your permission I will take this opportunity to commend you on the fine spirit of sportsmanship displayed by the men of your college on the eventful night of June third and its subsequent happenings. I trust that better understanding and not hard feeling grew out of it on both sides.*
>
> *Many of my friends and relatives have remarked how thoughtful it was of you to remember me in such a fine way. Needless to say I hold the opinion and wish to thank you once more for the beautiful flowers and the spirit that accompanied them.*
>
> *Should I ever be in a position to be of any service to you, it would indeed be a pleasure for me to perform what I might.*
>
> *Very sincerely yours,*
> *Charles G. Oakman*

Over time, the fountain fell into disrepair and was removed in 1961.

Chapter 14

Chief Connors Goes to Jail

At noon on Monday, June 18, 1928, John F. Connors, who had been the chief of police for the city of Ypsilanti for eight years, tendered his letter of resignation to the city police commission. The letter read, "I herewith tender my resignation as Chief of Police of the City of Ypsilanti, effective this date."

A meeting of the police commission was called immediately after Connors submitted his resignation, where it was accepted. Patrolman Coy Rankin was temporarily placed in charge of the department.

After the meeting, Connors said he had no statement to make concerning his resignation. Connors did say he had several other positions under consideration but had not made a decision.

Ypsilanti mayor Matthew Max and the members of the commission had no statement as well, other than that the resignation had been expected by the commission since the beginning of the new fiscal year. "At this time expenses of the past year were reviewed and reductions made in the budget for the coming year," noted the *Ypsilanti Daily Press* of Monday, June 18.

The events that led to the resignation of Connors began at the start of the new fiscal year, when Mayor Max appointed a budget committee to examine the records of each city department in an effort to reduce expenditures in the new fiscal year. When the committee examined the police fund, they found a Charles Hall on the payroll. Neither the mayor nor any member of the committee, Aldermen Burrell, Steffee or Ordway knew anything of this man Hall. The committee questioned Connors about the man. Connors told

Ypsilanti mayor Matthew Max appointed the budget committee that discovered the discrepancies in the funds of the police department. *Courtesy of the Ypsilanti Historical Society.*

the committee that Hall was an undercover man who he had brought into the city to carry out some investigating. His name had been on the payroll since October 3.

The committee was not entirely satisfied with the answers, as there were no records of any raids or arrests resulting from the work of this Hall. The committee also failed to find any member of the police department who was acquainted with Hall. The committee then summoned the members of the police commission, E.G. Wiedman, D.L. Quirk Jr. and Alfred Webber, for a consultation. Under the city charter, it was the duty of the commissioners to hire all members of the police department, and all vouchers for paychecks had to be signed by them.

The *Ypsilanti Daily Press* of July 2 noted:

They stated that they had not hired Hall, and did not know such a man, but that confidence in the police chief had led Commissioners Wiedman and Quirk to sign vouchers, authorizing the city clerk to make out the pay checks. Mr. Webber is a new member of the commission, appointed by Mayor Max at the beginning of the present fiscal year, and had no knowledge of any of the proceedings.

The commissioners informed the Mayor they had no reason to doubt Mr. Connors word that he had engaged Hall for under cover work. From time to time over a period of years they said, extra men had been on the police payroll. Regular officers known in the city cannot secure evidence against bootleggers or other suspected criminals, and it is a regular practice for police to engage under cover men to work in plain clothes. However, Hall was not engaged by the commissioners, and never took an oath of office before City Clerk Harvey Holmes, as regular patrolmen have customarily done, the committee learned.

At this time, it was the custom of the city clerk's office to give to the department head all the checks for that department. Then it was the responsibility of the department head to distribute the checks to the members of that department. This saved the city clerk's office the trouble of distributing several hundred checks from the office of the clerk to individuals. Under this practice, the city clerk had turned over to Connors the checks for Hall, as well as all the checks for the members of the police department. It further developed that all the checks made out to Hall had been cashed by Connors at the Ypsilanti Savings Bank. Connors had frequently presented more than one check at the bank at a time. These checks had been cashed without question, although many times the checks had not been countersigned by Connors.

Since the procedure was at the least irregular and there was nothing to show for the work of this Hall, who had been on the city payroll for eight months, Mayor Max continued his investigation. He found nine other names on the police department payroll for the previous two and a half years whom no one could account for. Nearly all these checks were for $75, payment for two weeks' work, and had been cashed in the same way. The total amount was between $3,600 and $4,000.

Mayor Max asked Connors to produce Hall, who was the most recent of the names to appear on the city payroll. Connors informed Mayor Max that Hall had been dismissed in May but could be produced. No action was taken, and finally Mayor Max informed Connors that he must produce Hall at a meeting of the budget committee and the police commissioner to be held at 4:30 p.m. on June 18.

Should Connors fail to produce Hall, then Mayor Max would be obliged to ask Connors for his resignation. It was at noon on that day that Connors tendered his resignation to E.G. Wiedman, chairman of the police commission.

"Since that time Mayor Max has continued to press for some action on the case. It was his contention that if no irregularity existed, Hall could be and should be produced, and the suspicion of embezzlement removed from the name of the former chief of police. If it was a case of embezzlement, he felt some settlement was due the city," noted the *Ypsilanti Daily Press.*

Finally, the case was brought to the attention of Washtenaw County assistant prosecutor Floyd Daggett, who carried out his own investigation.

Daggett found sufficient evident to bring the matter to the attention of Washtenaw County prosecuting attorney Carl Stuhrberg.

A warrant was issued charging Connors with obtaining money under false pretense on the afternoon of Monday, July 2. The arraignment was held on the morning of July 2 in the office of Justice D.Z. Curtiss. Connors appeared with his attorney, Louis Burk, and demanded an examination on the charge. The specific charge on which the warrant was issued was a check for $75 made out to Charles Hall on April 17, 1928. There was no discussion of the offense at the arraignment. The date for the examination was set for August 8, and bond was set at $5,000. The bond was furnished by Lee Dawson.

After several delays, the examination of Connors began on the morning of Thursday, December 6, 1928, before Justice A.J. Warren of Saline at the Ypsilanti City Hall. Warren was present as Ypsilanti justice D.Z. Curtiss had been subpoenaed as a witness.

Ypsilanti city clerk Harvey Holmes was called as a witness, and he explained the procedure by which city employees were paid. The head of each department made out the vouchers for the employees on the payroll, explained Holmes. These were signed by the commissioners and approved by the ways and means committee and then presented to the city council by the clerk for approval. Once this was approved by the council, the clerk made out the checks. The checks were dated the day of the council meeting, although they were not made out until the following morning.

The clerk's record of the council proceedings of the meeting when the check the case was based on was authorized was introduced as evidence to show that the bills were not passed singly but in one resolution that authorized the clerk to write the checks for "all bills properly signed by the commissioners and committees." The bills were "considered read and approved and orders drawn."

Holmes testified that he had never seen Hall and had never talked to Connors about Hall.

Testimony in the case resumed on Thursday, December 20, because attorneys for Connors could not be present in court before then. The chief witness heard that day was handwriting expert Francis B. Courtney, who had been secured to examine the check in question and other documents on which the handwriting of Connors appeared. Courtney testified that the signature of Charles Hall appearing as an endorsement on the check on which the complaint was based and the signature on another check, "Charles Gore by John Connors," were the same. Courtney said he had examined in all seventy-nine checks and eight or ten documents bearing

Left: Former Ypsilanti mayor E. Van de Walker signed the check to Charles Hall that came into question. *Courtesy of the Ypsilanti Historical Society.*

Below: The Savings Bank building where Chief Connors cashed the checks made out to Hall. *Courtesy of the Ypsilanti Historical Society.*

the handwriting of Connors. He declared his positive opinion that the writing was all the same, with an obvious attempt to disguise the writing on the Charles Hall check.

"Courtney's testimony was attacked by counsel for Connors on the grounds that it was the opinion of one man which might be wrong, and that he had spent only from 10 a.m. to 3 p.m. examining the handwriting," noted the *Ypsilanti Daily Press* of Thursday, December 20.

In the end, Justice Warren ordered Connors bound over to the next term of the circuit court for immediate trial. Bond was set at $5,000.

The case did not go to trial immediately, as the attorneys for Connors could not come to court. One, Louis Burk, motioned for a continuance of the case to the March term because attorney George Burk was in Florida recovering from an operation. Washtenaw County Circuit Court judge George W. Sample delayed the case to the March term.

The *Ypsilanti Daily Press* of Wednesday, March 6, 1929, reported:

> *Two weeks ago, attorneys for Connors met members of the council and offered a settlement of $2,000. The council unanimously refused to accept that amount and notified the police commissioners of the move which had been made towards a financial settlement, suggesting that they give consideration to determining what might be a fair and reasonable settlement, in view of the fact that there is some question concerning whether any of the doubtful checks Connors had made out from the police payroll were bona fide.*

At the council meeting of Monday, March 4, the police commissioners submitted their report, which read: "Your commissioners met at the First National Bank at 1 o'clock Wednesday afternoon and after an extended discussion of the above matter, resolved that no recommendation could be made. We do not have the handling of the funds nor any of the financial end of the work, and since the matter rests with the council, we feel justified in reaching our conclusion."

The council accepted the report of the commissioners but was not happy with it. In the curt words of Mayor Matthew Max, "If they had not signed those vouchers, we wouldn't have paid them."

On the morning of Tuesday, March 5, Connors was arraigned before Judge George Sample and pleaded not guilty to the charge of obtaining money under false pretenses. That same morning, before the arraignment, an effort was made to raise additional funds to offer to the city as a settlement. The mayor and council agreed to allow the hearing to be placed on the circuit

The First National Bank Building where the police commissioners held their meeting and "resolved that no recommendation could be made." *Courtesy of the Ypsilanti Historical Society.*

court calendar for March 25, 1929. This gave the attorneys for Connors more time to arrange a settlement that the city would see as reasonable. The *Ypsilanti Daily Press* of Thursday, March 21, reported:

> *At a special meeting of city council Wednesday evening, seven aldermen, representing the city agreed to accept the last offer of financial settlement made by Connors. By its terms the city receives $2,750 in cash and two years notes, bearing 6 per cent interest and endorsed by local men, for $1,825. The money was to be turned over by Louis Burk, attorney for John Connors, only with the understanding that the city informs the prosecuting attorney, Carl Stuhrberg, that the settlement has been made and agree that he should recommend to the county circuit judge George W. Sample, that the case be dropped.*

Under the terms of the agreement, the city would have no further claims on Connors, and Connors would have no claims on the city. Connors agreed to turn over the money only with the understanding that the city drop the case. Connors never pleaded guilty to the crime, and the case would stand as dropped. Under the agreement, the city would accept the money "in payment of the debt owing the city."

All that was left was for Judge Sample to agree to the deal.

As agreed, on Thursday, March 21, Prosecuting Attorney Carl Stuhrberg presented Judge Sample with a certified copy of the action of the city council when it accepted the deal. The only problem was Judge Sample did not accept the deal.

"The action of the city council Ypsilanti, nor the whole city of Ypsilanti for that matter, will not sway the court one iota from the path of Justice," said Sample in a statement. "I have notified the prosecutor's office to be prepared to start the trial of John Connors Monday."

On the morning of Monday, March 25, attorneys for John Connors, Louis Burk and George Burk, appeared before Judge Sample and informed him that they had withdrawn from the case. They asked for a two-week adjournment so Connors could secure new legal representation. Louis Burk explained that Connors believed he could secure Lester Moll, former assistant prosecutor of Wayne County, in that time. Sample denied the motion and ordered Connors to appear before the court that afternoon at 3:00 p.m. Sample said if Connors had not secured counsel by that time, Sample would appoint an attorney for him.

Moll appeared as attorney for Connors that afternoon and filed a motion for a change of venue because of the publicity the case had received in the local newspapers. Sample denied the motion, saying the papers "were bound to print the developments and content of the news, and that he could see no breach of good faith in their conduct so far.

"I can see no reason," said Sample, "why this case should go out of this community for trial; it should be tried in this court if possible. I believe a jury can be chosen without one iota of prejudice in one way or another. The question to be settled does not deal with Connors' offer of settlement to the city of Ypsilanti, but of his guilt or innocence of the criminal charges of obtaining money under false pretense."

Moll filed a motion for a continuance of the case, as he had not had sufficient time to prepare. He asked that the case be held over to the May 1929 term of the court. Sample denied this motion as well.

A jury was selected on the morning of Friday, March 29. The jury of thirteen men and one woman was sworn to sit on the case, and the court then adjourned until 3:00 p.m. of that afternoon in observance of Good Friday.

Once the court reconvened, Prosecutor Stuhrberg made a brief opening statement lasting less than ten minutes. He said the people would prove that beginning in September 1925, Connors had "placed the names of several non-existing men on the payroll of the police department, twice each month, that these two checks each month were drawn for $75 or under, and that they were all endorsed by John Connors, who got the money."

Moll made no secret of his plan to base his defense of Connors on his record as chief of police:

Our principal defense is John Connors himself. Practically and substantially we shall show that he is an orderly citizen who has lived and worked among you, who is approaching 50 years of age, and whose record as a citizen and public official is without blemish—and beyond reproach.

The defense will further show how Connors was vested with authority to employ or discharge members of the department, and how he regarded his duties not only as those of apprehending criminals, but of preserving the general peace of the community. Mr. Connors gave thought to the prevention and investigation of the sources of crime and in this he often needed outside assistance.

The first witness called to the stand was City Clerk Harvey Holmes, who took the stand while holding a suitcase. The suitcase contained the cancelled checks, vouchers and other items of evidence. The prosecutor introduced all seventy-seven checks into evidence, over the objection of the defense. The defense stated that only the one check on which charges against Connors had been brought could be introduced, as all the others were "incompetent, irrelevant and immaterial."

Seven of the checks introduced by the prosecutor were in the name of Ivan Keefer, twenty-one in the name of James Ross, ten in the name of Leonard Schnell, nine in the name of George Buland and fifteen in the name of Charles Gore. All the checks bore the proper signatures of the city clerk and the mayor. The vouchers bore those of the chief of police, the city clerk and the members of the ways and means commissions. Endorsements of each of the checks were in the name of the payee, "by John F. Connors."

Court adjourned while Holmes was still on the stand and resumed on the morning of Tuesday, April 2. At this time, Holmes produced the rest of the questioned checks, as well as Connors's oath of office, dated December 1, 1919, and Connors's letter of resignation, dated June 18, 1928. Holmes also produced a record of the proceeding of the common council of its meeting of June 18, 1928, when the resignation of Connors was accepted.

Under cross-examination, Holmes said he had never seen any of the "under-cover" men in question. Holmes admitted he had not personally known Arthur Lambert, who had joined the department from June 1, 1926, until June 1928. When asked if he could be sure Charles Hall had ever been employed by the city, Holmes answered, "I do not know."

The next witness was Francis B. Courtney, the handwriting expert. Courtney testified that on each of the checks paid to alleged nonexistent men, he had detected an "attempt to disguise" the writing of Connors.

The Quirk House on North Huron Street was Ypsilanti City Hall from 1913 to 1970. During those years, many important decisions were made, including those concerning the fate of Chief of Police John Connors. *Courtesy of the Ypsilanti Historical Society.*

On Wednesday, April 3, Arthur Lambert testified he had known and worked with Ivan Kiefer, one of the alleged undercover men in question, on the liquor situation in Ypsilanti before Lambert became a regular member of the Ypsilanti Police Department in June 1926. Lambert said he and Kiefer had worked together to secure evidence in liquor cases. During the time he had worked as an undercover man, Lambert said he had been paid $77.50 in cash. The check was produced, and it was endorsed, "Arthur Lambert, by John Connors." Lambert had resigned from the Ypsilanti Police Department a few weeks before the trial to become a member of the Detroit Police Department.

Connors took the stand in his own defense. In answer to a direct question, Connors said, "I have never defrauded or attempted to defraud the city of Ypsilanti."

Connors said he got the idea of using undercover men from an inspector of the Detroit police. He said he made every effort to find Charles Hall, even

110

making trips to Detroit and Chicago, where he searched both police and underworld channels without success.

Connors said he had endorsed all the checks to the undercover men himself as a precaution to keep anyone in the city from knowing who they were. He said he met the men in various places, including city hall in the evening, at which time he gave them their pay in cash. Connors stated he had led many raids on the strength of the information furnished by the undercover men. This information concerned not only bootleggers but also perpetrators of more serious crimes such as holdups and robberies.

The case went to the jury before noon on Friday, April 5. The jury returned a verdict of "guilty as charged" after deliberation of approximately three and a half hours.

Once the verdict was rendered, Connors was taken to the Washtenaw County Jail, where he remained until the morning of Saturday, April 13, when he was taken before Judge Sample to hear his sentence passed. When called by the court to hear sentence pronounced, Connors walked to the bench with a firm step. When asked if he had anything to say, Connors said, "All I have to say, your honor, is that I am innocent of the crime with which I am charged."

When Judge Sample pronounced sentence, he said, "I know of no more serious crime than that of a public official who betrays the trust placed in him. It is my personal belief that you are guilty. I am satisfied that the jury was right." Judge Sample sentenced Connors to five to ten years in the Michigan State Reformatory at Ionia. Judge Sample further ordered Connors to pay a fine of $1,000.

Judge Sample then recommended that Connors serve five years in prison and then reduced this to two and a half years, should Connors make restitution to the city. The amount set by the city was $4,575, in addition to the fine of $1,000.

Connors was taken from the Washtenaw County Jail on the morning of Wednesday, April 17, and transported to the reformatory at Ionia. Riding in the car with Connors were two other prisoners, one sentenced to two and a half to ten years on a "statutory charge" and the other sentenced to one and a half to fifteen years for his part in a robbery.

Attorneys for Connors filed a motion for a new trial and an application for a writ of error to the Michigan State Supreme Court on Tuesday, April 23. The *Ypsilanti Daily Press* of Wednesday, April 24, reported:

> *Grounds for asking a new trial include 37 points being based principally on a belief that the court erred in instructing the jury. Two minor points in the*

prosecutor's argument to the jury were cited. The motion states that the court erred in refusing a change of venue, that it was prejudiced in imposing a fine on the respondent in the sum of $1,000 and that it did not discharge the respondent on grounds that testimony taken in examination was not on file with the county clerk at the time the information was filed. Grounds upon which the new trial is asked cover 16 typewritten pages.

Connors was released from Ionia on bond on June 11, 1929, pending the outcome of the appeal. The Supreme Court of Michigan announced its decision on June 2, 1930. The court unanimously confirmed the conviction of Connors.

"On this record," noted the court, "a jury could not well have returned any verdict except that of guilty. Remaining questions have been considered, and, as it appears there has been no miscarriage of justice, we think the judgment should be affirmed."

Connors had to return to Ionia to serve out his sentence.

Chapter 15

A Roar in Depot Town

God's Children

The fortunes of the section of Ypsilanti known today as Depot Town have always been tied to the prosperity of the railroad. Ever since the arrival of the first train in February 1838, this section of the city has been dependent on the money the railroad attracted. When the railroads went into decline, this section of the city felt the loss and by the late 1960s had become the unsavory part of the city. This was the part of town fathers told their daughters to stay out of. This section of the city had been in decline for some time, and the presences of God's Children did not help. God's Children did not sing in the choir but were a motorcycle gang, an offshoot of Hell's Angels.

God's Children motorcycle gang was founded as a club in January 1967 and set up headquarters at 25½ East Cross Street soon after. The gang stayed out of trouble until the Fourth of July 1967, when it threatened to invade the Happyland Shows carnival in Waterworks Park and "tear the place up."

For a number of years, the city of Ypsilanti had celebrated the Fourth of July with a carnival at Waterworks Park. The fun at the carnival was marred in 1967 by racial trouble. According to police, a member of the gang had been assaulted by a group of African Americans on Sunday, July 2, and the members of God's Children gathered at the carnival on Tuesday, July 4, to "even the score."

Police arrested two members of the gang after heavy chains were found in the back window of their car. Two other members of the gang were arrested when police found heavy chains with padlocks wrapped around their waists.

Police forced open the trunk of a car belonging to a member of the gang and found fifteen Molotov cocktails (fire bombs), a wire whip with fishhooks attached to the ends of the wires, heavy chains, a fish spear, an umbrella with a spear taped to the tip, a small pronged garden hoe and wooden and metal clubs.

Four members of the club were charged with carrying dangerous weapons, and two of them, along with six other members of the gang, were charged with conspiracy to incite a public disturbance. A total of eleven gang members were charged by police.

"Several of the motorcyclists, after being herded into the garage at the police station to await booking, damaged a heavy overhead door, trying to open it. Police Chief Ray H. Walton said he didn't know whether any escaped because of the large number in the room," reported the *Ypsilanti Press* of Wednesday, July 5. Several members of the gang were sentenced to time in jail for their actions.

That same month saw the first gang wedding, which the mother of the groom described as "different." The wedding was held in the backyard of the parents of the groom. The parents of the bride were not in attendance, as it was explained that "they're working."

"The groom, wearing an Iron Cross, motorcycle boots and a blue denim vest that left his chest bare, walked with his bride to the shade of some box elder trees. She wore a pink and white dress and flats," reported the *Ypsilanti Press* of July 22.

The groom said he had taken the day off from work as a pump press operator at the Ford Motor Company Rawsonville plant.

"The backyard ceremony Saturday afternoon was brief," noted the account. "The proper words were said. The couple kissed. Then someone said the rings had been forgotten. That matter attended to the couple kissed again."

The couple embraced, and the club members chanted, "Children! Children!"

The couple was married by the Reverend Kenneth J. Smith of the First Pilgrim Church. "I hadn't known about this," said the Reverend Smith later. "But I should have guessed they'd all be there.

"They were very respectful," he added. "There was no discourtesy whatsoever."

The father of the groom showed the club members how his bullwhip worked as everyone sat around drinking and talking.

"The newlyweds smiled," the account concluded. "It was their day."

The gang members enjoyed riding their motorcycles on the unpaved trails on the then-undeveloped land around Ford Lake. When not riding their motorcycles, the members would stop and take part in other physical activities. Young boys observing from the safety of tree limbs learned things their parents would not have wanted them to know at that age.

Members of God's Children, as well as members of the Spokemen of Dearborn and the Huns of Detroit, spent the afternoon of Sunday, May 5, 1968, "scrambling on the dirt roads near the lake." As they were returning to Ypsilanti at about 7:00 p.m., the riders found themselves following a car on Grove Road near Jay Avenue. The car in front of the riders was forced to stop suddenly when the car in front of it slowed to make a turn.

The riders coming up behind the car attempted to avoid a rear-end collision. As the riders did so, a young woman on the back of one of the motorcycles apparently struck her knee against the car and was thrown off.

"Ypsilanti Township Justice of the Peace John B. Collins who was turning into his driveway about 300 feet from the accident scene, ran into his home to phone the [Michigan State Police] post, while a nurse who was with him drove over to assist the girl," reported the *Ypsilanti Press* of Saturday, May 11.

At about this time, another witness phoned the Michigan State Police Post to report "a large group of cyclists beating up on a man."

Michigan state police officer John V. Shewell arrived alone but was joined minutes later by two state police cruisers and four Washtenaw County Sheriff Department cars. Officer Shewell later said he asked the group of riders to stand aside so he could investigate the accident. At this, Shewell said, the cyclists began to shout and curse at him. Those who saw the incident said later there were eight to thirteen motorcycles and about sixteen individuals at the scene.

"Witnesses said the cyclists, men and women, were shouting, screaming and cursing the trooper, demanding that the officer, trying to sort out the incident, only look after the injured girl," noted the account.

The riders said the girl who had been thrown off the motorcycle had a broken leg. She was later treated at Beyer Memorial Hospital and released with no apparent serious injuries.

"Witnesses said at first she was lying on the ground, but soon sat up and smoked a cigarette while the furor went on," noted the account.

One man was arrested by Officer Shewell when the man swore in the presence of women. When Officer Shewell tried to search the man, a second rider moved toward Officer Shewell. The man Officer Shewell was trying to search broke away, and another rider grabbed Officer Shewell by the throat. Officer Shewell threw the one man off him and then pulled out his blackjack and hit the other. The man who had held Officer Shewell fled. Three men were arrested and charged with being disorderly persons, assault and carrying concealed weapons.

God's Children caused little trouble in Depot Town itself, but their presence was intimidating. Some objected to their running naked in the street, while others said this was an improvement. Those who looked in the windows of the Central Bar, it is said, risked being beaten. For Depot Town to flourish, God's Children had to go. Residents sought ways to encourage the gang to move on.

On the night of July 18, 1971, someone dropped an explosive device down a chimney of the building where their clubhouse was. The explosive device apparently caught halfway down the chimney. The device exploded at 11:53 p.m. and did considerable damage to the second and third floors of the building. At the time of the explosion, there were eight to ten persons in the clubroom, but none was injured. "Club members," reported the *Ypsilanti Press* of July 19, "told police they didn't know anything about the incident."

According to local legend, the gang said this did not scare them and that they were not leaving. The gang then left on a vacation from which they have yet to return.

Once the gang was gone, the urban pioneers who had settled in the neighborhood and were investing their time and money in the old buildings and new businesses took over. A new age had begun.

Bibliography

First Murder

Ann Arbor Journal. "The Circuit Court." June 20, 1860.

————. "The Circuit Court." June 27, 1860.

————. "Crime and Causality in Ypsilanti." May 30, 1860.

Chapman, Charles C. *History of Washtenaw County.* Chicago: Chas. C. Chapman & Co., 1881.

Cooley, Thomas M. *Michigan Reports: Reports of Cases Heard and Decided in the Michigan Supreme Court of Michigan the Beginning of April Term, 1862, to November 13, 1862.* Vol. VI.

Detroit Free Press. "Supposed Murder at Ypsilanti." May 23, 1860.

Dead Man Alive

"Record of Service of Michigan Volunteers in the Civil War." Published by authority of the Senate and House of Representatives of the Michigan Legislature, under the direction of Brigadier General Geo. H. Brown, Adjutant General.

Ypsilanti Commercial. "Condition of the South—Southern Revenge—Our Poor, Suffering, Brave Soldier Boys." January 30, 1869.

————. "A Dead Man Comes to Life." January 23, 1869.

————. "The 'Lost Son.'" March 20, 1869.

————. March 10, 1877.

TEMPERANCE WAR OF 1873

Michigan Argus. "Ypsilanti Items." August 8, 1873.

Ypsilanti Commercial. "Another Chapter." October 18, 1873.

————. "Another Turn of the Wheel." November 22, 1873.

————. "Council Proceedings." August 9, 1873.

————. "Council Proceedings." August 30, 1873.

————. "Council Proceedings." July 26, 1873.

————. "Extracts from Our City Charter Relating to the Temperance Question." March 8, 1873.

————. "Inaugural Address." May 9, 1874.

————. "An Invasion." May 21, 1874.

————. "Justice Crane." December 13, 1873.

————. "Justice Warner." November 29, 1873.

————. "The Latest Attempts to Fire the City." August 9, 1873.

————. "Marvelous Events, Tremendous Excitement." August 16, 1873.

————. "Myron Brown." August 23, 1873.

————. "Myron Brown." May 30, 1874.

————. "An Ordinance." January 31, 1873.

————. "An Ordinance Relative to Disorderly Houses and Houses of Ill Fame." August 2, 1873.

————. "The People vs. Albert Grant." November 1, 1873.

————. "The People vs. E. Bortle." March 21, 1874.

————. "The People vs. John Martin." October 11, 1873.

————. "People vs. Martin Eckrick." January 31, 1874.

————. "The Recent Outrages." July 26, 1873.

————. "Two True Chapters in the History of Ypsilanti." May 30, 1874.

————. "Whiskey." February 8, 1873.

————. "William Keatling." October 25, 1873.

————. "Wonderful Disclosure." December 20, 1873.

Body in the Cistern

Detroit Free Press. "Drown in a Cistern." December 23, 1873.
————. "More Mystery." December 24, 1873.
Peninsular Courier. "A Mysterious Case." January 2, 1874.
Ypsilanti Commercial. "May Robinson." December 27, 1873.

A Serenade for Editor Pattison

Chapman, Charles C. *History of Washtenaw County.* Chicago: Chas. C. Chapman & Co., 1881.
Colburn, Harvey C. *The Story of Ypsilanti.* N.p., 1923.
Ypsilanti Commercial. "A Republican Mob." November 5, 1886.

Ypsilanti Excited

Ann Arbor Daily Argus. "Was Sentenced for 20 Years." October 3, 1901.
Ann Arbor Register. "A Bold Robbery." February 3, 1894.
Washtenaw Evening Times. "The Coroner's Inquest." February 23, 1894.
————. "No Trace of Bill Jones." February 20, 1894.
————. "Shot Himself Dead!" February 22, 1894.
————. "Ypsilanti Is Excited." February 19, 1894.
The Ypsilantian. "Bad Brothers." February 22, 1894.
Ypsilanti Commercial. "Shot the Officer." February 23, 1894.

A Woman Saved by Her Corset

Daily Ypsilanti Press. "Death Summons Thomas H. Ninde." February 24, 1926.
Evening Times. "Must Suffer." October 8, 1898.
————. October 4, 1898.
————. "Through Jealousy." October 3, 1898.
Ypsilantian. "An Outbreak of Crime." October 6, 1898.

DEATHS OF COX AND CAMP

Ann Arbor Daily Argus. "Body of Wm. Cox Was Laid to Rest." October 28, 1905.

————. "Double Suicide or Murder Case." October 26, 1905.

————. "It Means Nothing." November 4, 1905.

————. "The Signature Is Important." October 27, 1905.

Ann Arbor Daily Times. "Couple's Illicit Love Ends in Awful Tragedy." October 26, 1905.

————. "They Insist on Murder Theory." October 27, 1905.

————. "Was It Murder or Suicide?" November 4, 1905.

Detroit Free Press. "Illicit Love Ended in the Death of Two." October 26, 1905.

————. "Not a Suicide." October 27, 1905.

Detroit News. "Officials Roast Cox-Camp Verdict." November 4, 1905.

————. "Suspects Murder in Ypsi. Tragedy." October 26, 1905.

Ypsilanti Daily Press. "Believes It Was Murder." October 27, 1905.

————. "Bodies of Man and Woman." October 25, 1905.

————. "Cox Suicide, Camp Murder." November 4, 1905.

————. "Was a Crime Committed?" October 26, 1905.

BAD START TO 1909

Ann Arbor Daily News. "Stabbed His Wife Then Fled and Was Killed by M.C. Train." January 2, 1909.

Ypsilanti Daily Press. "Says That Klavitter Committed Suicide." January 14, 1909.

————. "Stabbed Wife and Killed Self." January 2, 1909.

A CRIME OF SUNDAY BASEBALL

Ypsilanti Daily Press. "Aldermen Leave Baseball Question in the Air Till Election." August 20, 1912.

————. "A.M. Henne, Manager Ypsi Opera House, to Be Tried Friday." September 3, 1912.

————. "City Attorney Brown Loses 3d Case." September 7, 1912.

————. "Committee to Adjust Base Ball Ordinance." August 6, 1912.

————. "Mayor Norton Orders Arrest of Ypsi Baseball Team." July 15, 1912.

————. "Mayor Still 'Game' Orders Another Arrest." July 31, 1912.

————. "Rank Conditions Confronting Mayor Norton Emphasized by Second Base Ball Trial." August 2, 1912.

————. "Well Picked Jury Thwarts Mayor's Effort to Enforce Base Ball Law in Ypsilanti." July 26, 1912.

Throwing Eggs at the "Escaped Nun"

Daily Ypsilanti Press. "Egg Throwing Not Approved by Catholic Club Women." March 5, 1920.

————. "Egg Throwing to Be Investigated." March 3, 1920.

————. "'Escaped Nun' Files Suit for Heavy Damage." March 18, 1920.

————. "Threw Eggs in Church Meeting." March 2, 1920.

Ypsilanti Record. "Eggs Thrown in F.M. Church." March 4, 1920.

Smoking Scandal at the Normal

Ann Arbor Times. "Attorneys Sill File Briefs in Cigarette Issue." June 14, 1922.

————. "Pres. Burton on Stand in Cigarette Suit." June 13, 1922.

Cooper, Richard W. *Michigan Reports: Cases Decided in the Supreme Court of Michigan from January 7 to April 10, 1924.* Chicago: Callaghan and Company, 1931.

Daily Ypsilanti Press. "Alice Tanton Tells Court of 'Indiscretions.'" June 13, 1922.

————. "Believe Court Will Sustain Normal Stand." June 14, 1922.

————. "Detroit Co-Ed Sues to Be Returned to Normal." April 18, 1922.

————. "Governor Calls for Probe of Normal; M'Kenny Makes Reply." April 18, 1922.

————. "Judge Sample Upholds Rules of the Normal." September 9, 1922.

————. "Matrons Assn. Stands Behind Faculty Order." April 20, 1922.

————. "M'Kenny Upheld by State Board Here Saturday." May 1, 1922.

————. "Pres. McKenny Defends the Modern Girl and Her Dress." February 25, 1922.

————. "17 Girl Smokers Are Ousted from Normal." April 12, 1922.
————. "Student Body Backs Action of College." April 19, 1922.
————. "Take Ten More Days on Brief." June 23, 1922.
Detroit News. "Co-Ed Smoker a Hit on Stand." June 13, 1922.
————. "17 Ypsi Co-Eds Fired for Violating Rules." April 12, 1922.
Isbell, Egbert R. *A History of Eastern Michigan University, 1849–1965.* Ypsilanti: Eastern Michigan University Press, 1971.
New York Times. "Michigan College Sends 17 Girls Home." April 13, 1922.
Normal College News. "President McKenny Issues Statement." April 2, 1922.
Ypsilanti Daily Press. "Help of Women Who Keep Roomers Is Solicited." July 29, 1912.
————. "If We Must Sacrifice Our Parlors Pres. M'Kenney Should Provide Means for Pay, Says Landlady." July 30, 1912.
————. "Landladies Not Anxious for Chaperon Job." August 3, 1912.
————. "President Puts Ban on Public Parties." July 24, 1912.

FRACAS AT THE FOUNTAIN

Daily Ypsilanti Press. "Normal Men Clash with U of M Visitors." June 4, 1925.
————. "Normal Students Wait in Vain for War Like Invaders Expected from Ann Arbor." June 5, 1925.
Normal College News. "Ann Arbor Battle Is Not Repeated." June 12, 1925.
————. "Ann Arbor Invades Ypsilanti Campus." June 5, 1925.
————. "Fountain Fracas 'Closed Episode.'" June 12, 1925.

CHIEF CONNORS GOES TO JAIL

Cooper, Richard W. *Michigan Reports: Cases Decided in the Supreme Court of Michigan from June 2 to October 3, 1930.* Vol. 251. Chicago: Callaghan and Company, 1931.
Ypsilanti Daily Press. "Attorneys for Ex-Police Head to Appeal Case." April 6, 1929.
————. "Burkes Withdraw from Connors Defense." March 25, 1929.
————. "Chief of Police Resigns." June 18, 1928.
————. "Circuit Court Trial of Connors Case Ordered." December 20, 1928.

————. "City Accepts $4,575 Connors Case Settlement." March 21, 1929.

————. "Connors Admits Endorsing Hall Checks." April 2, 1929.

————. "Connors Asks New Trial, Writ of Error." April 24, 1929.

————. "Connors Case Goes to Jury before Noon." April 5, 1929.

————. "Connors Conviction Upheld." June 2, 1930.

————. "Connors Given 5–10 Years in Ionia." April 13, 1929.

————. "Connors Jury Sworn, Testimony to Start." March 29, 1929.

————. "Connors' Record as Police Chief Will Be Defense." March 30 1929.

————. "Connors Released on Bond of Five Thousand." July 3, 1928.

————. "Connors Settlement." March 6, 1929.

————. "Connors Taken to Ionia Today." April 17, 1929.

————. "Connors' 'Under Cover' Man Known." April 3, 1929.

————. "J. Connors Hearing Started. December 6, 1928.

————. "John F. Connors, Ex Police Chief Charged with Mis-Appropriating City Funds, Warrant Issued." July 2, 1928.

————. "Prosecutor Not Satisfied with Connors Delays." December 13, 1928.

————. "Testimony Ends in Connors' Fraud Trial." April 4, 1929.

A ROAR IN DEPOT TOWN: GOD'S CHILDREN

Ypsilanti Press. "Attempted Bombing Is Probed." July 19, 1971.

————. "Cycle Gangs Attack Trooper." May 6, 1968.

————. "11 Cyclists Charged in Carnival Trouble." July 5, 1967.

————. "Groom Wears Iron Cross to Wed." July 22, 1967.

————. "Motorcycle Quartet Gets Jail, Probation." April 2, 1968.

————. "Rough Treatment Claimed by Cyclists." May 11, 1968.

About the Author

James Thomas Mann is a local historian, storyteller and author in Ypsilanti, Michigan. His books include *Ypsilanti: A History in Pictures*; *Ypsilanti in the 20th Century*; *City of Ypsilanti Fire Department 100 Years*; *Footnotes in History*; and *Our Heritage: Down by the Depot in Ypsilanti*. His previous books for The History Press are *Wicked Washtenaw County* and *Wicked Ann Arbor*.